SMALL SPACE
GARDENING
—for—
CANADA

Laura Peters

LONE
PINE

Lone Pine Publishing
2311–96 Street
Edmonton, AB T6N 1G3
Canada

Website: www.lonepinepublishing.com

Library and Archives Canada Cataloguing in Publication

Peters, Laura, 1968-
    Small space gardening for Canada / Laura Peters.

ISBN 978-1-55105-860-3

    1. Urban gardening. 2. Small gardens. I. Title.

SB453.P47 2012   635.091732   C2011-908560-7

Editorial Director: Nancy Foulds
Project Editor: Sheila Quinlan
Production Manager: Gene Longson
Layout and Production: Janina Kürschner
Cover Design: Gerry Dotto

Photography: All photos are by Sandy Weatherall except: Sandra Bit 40b, 85a; Tamara Eder, 46, 82, 101, 106, 107, 110, 112a, 123, 163a, 167, 169, 173; iStock 1, 83a, 112b, 118, 119; Liz Klose 152, 153; L. Lauzuma 145; Suzanne Lewis 120a&b; Janet Loughrey 166; Tim Matheson 61a, 81a, 111, 113, 114, 115, 117, 162, 168; Laura Peters 30, 35b, 40a, 43, 44, 60a, 61b, 62, 63, 77, 83b, 84, 93, 94, 97a&b, 98, 99, 102b, 104, 109, 130, 133, 136, 149, 151a&b, 155, 156, 157, 158, 159b, 160, 161a&b, 163b, 165a, 170, 172; photos.com 75, 80, 81b, 108, 116; Proven Winners 164, 165b, 171; Robert Ritchie 105b; Nanette Samol 31, 41, 78, 79, 86, 87, 88, 89, 91all, 92, 95, 96, 102a, 103, 134, 137a&b, 138, 140, 144, 148, 150, 154; Paul Swanson 135b, 139a&b, 141; Peter Thompstone 159a; Mark Turner 146, 147.

Cover image: Liz Klose

Maps (p. 48): adapted from Natural Resources Canada

We acknowledge the financial support of the Government of Canada through the Canada Book Fund (CBF) for our publishing activities.

PC: 1

Table of Contents

Acknowledgements 6

Introduction 7

Why Bother? 10

Finding a Garden Space 13

Finding Space at Home 14
    Common Spaces 15
    Corridors and Stairways 19
    Rooftop Gardening .20
    Vertical Gardening 22
Finding Space Farther from Home 24
    Community Gardens .25
    Gardening at School or Work 29
    Urban Farming 30
    Guerilla Gardening .32

Optimizing Your Garden Space 33

Ideas and Inspiration 33
    Containers for Railings, Windowsills and Fences 35
    Hanging and Upside-down Gardens 36
    Vertical Planters 37
    Standard and Tiered Raised Beds 39
    Collapsible Containers 40
    Recycled Containers and Other Eclectic Innovations . . .40
Focus and Style 41
    The Importance of Focus 43
Evaluating Your Garden Space 45
    Climate and Microclimate 46
    Light 49
    Exposure 50
    Pollution 51
    Space 52
    Weight 53
Containers vs. Raised Beds 54
    The Pros and Cons of Containers 55

Container Materials 59
    Clay 59
    Wood 60
    Stone 61
    Metal 62
    Synthetics 63
Self-watering Containers 64
Making Your Own Self-watering Container 64
    The Materials 64
    The Assembly 64
The Pros and Cons of Raised Beds 67
Building Your Own Raised Bed 69
    The Materials 75
    The Build 75

Planting and Maintaining Your Garden Space   78

Tools for Urban Gardeners 78
    Tools for Digging 79
    Tools for Pruning 82
    Tools for Watering 83
    Tools for Supporting Your Plants 84
    Tools for Your Comfort 86
Preparing to Plant Your Container Garden 87
    Container Cleaning 87
    Container Drainage 88
    Choosing an Appropriate Planting Mix 88
    Reducing the Weight of Your Containers 90
Planting Your Container Garden 91
    Planting Trees and Specimen Plants 93
Container Garden Maintenance 94
    Watering 94
    Feeding 95
    Weeding 96
    Grooming 97
    Relieving Soil Compaction 99
    Repotting Plants 99
Preparing Your Container Garden for Winter 100
    Protecting Tender Plants 100

Storing Containers. 101
Insulating Containers. 102
Overwintering Hardy Plants 103
Overwintering Tender Rhizomes,
    Bulbs, Corms and Tubers 104
Pests and Diseases in Your Container Garden 104
Prevention and Control 106
The Importance of Water Conservation. 108
Mulch 109
The Importance of Compost 110
The Basics 111
Getting Started 113
Anaerobic Composting. 118
    Method One 118
    Method Two 119
Vermicomposting 120
A Final Word on Compost 121

The Plants   **122**

Edibles 122
Vegetables and Fruits 123
Herbs 125
Annuals 127
Perennials 130
Trees and Shrubs 132
Tropicals 132
The Top Threes 133
Top Three Vegetables 134
Top Three Fruits 144
Top Three Herbs 150
Top Three Annuals. 156
Top Three Perennials 162
Top Three Trees and Shrubs 167
Top Three Tropicals 170

Appendix: Companion Plants   **173**

About the Author   **176**

Acknowledgements

I would like to thank my parents, Gary and Lucy Peters, and my extended family of dear friends for their support and understanding when my life goes crazy because "She's writing another gardening book." It's often a blur of months, locked in my office, writing, searching for gardens to photograph and connecting with other gardeners, all of which I love. If it weren't for those who offer up their eclectic, special, lovingly tended and glorious garden spaces for us to photograph, we'd be lost and the books would be without a soul. So fellow gardeners, I thank you for your generosity and enthusiasm. I would also like to thank Sandy Weatherall, whose creativity, talent, skill, enthusiasm and positive personality have made this book more beautiful than I thought possible. It has been a genuine pleasure working with you, and I look forward to seeing more of your "artsy fartsy" garden images in the years to come. And thank you to everyone involved in making this the helpful guide that it is. I hope people with small and challenging spaces use it for years to come. Finally, as always, be generous to your garden and your garden will be generous in return.

Introduction

Chances are pretty good that if you've chosen this book as a gardening resource, you reside in an urban setting with very little to no green space of your own. You probably have a balcony, patio or deck, maybe an outdoor stairwell or rooftop, and you certainly have window-sills. You might even have a tiny back-yard in front of or behind a townhouse, just big enough for a bistro set, a barbe-cue, maybe a shrub and a small raised bed for growing vegetables or a tiny plot of perennials. But you most likely do not have an expansive backyard with nothing but space. Often the apartment, condo, townhouse and small home dwellers are forgotten in the gardening world, and the reason why has always been a mystery to me; after all, a large percentage of people in cities reside in these types of homes, including myself.

Thankfully for those of us who do not live in the traditional setting of a large house with a big yard, gardening is still a very real possibility. Not having large, expansive spaces shouldn't pre-vent urban dwellers from gardening for fun or for the rewards it can offer, regard-less of where in Canada you call home, how much space you have or what level of gardening skills you possess.

You don't need to have a yard to have a garden.

This type (and yes, it is a type) of gardening is currently known by a variety of names, but each one comes down to basically the same thing: growing plants in small spaces. There are simply different theories and methods as to the best way to do so. You'll see terms such as urban gardening, intensive gardening, square-foot gardening, vertical gardening, rooftop gardening and so on. Each method touches upon a growing trend.

Canadian cities are growing. With little land available, and profits a priority, houses are being built close together on small lots, and condominium complexes are becoming more and more common, often resulting in people being on top of one another and having little to no outdoor space of their own. Sure there are still heaps of houses with huge backyards that can more than accommodate a vegetable garden and flower beds, but in new developments, this setting has become increasingly rare.

For gardeners, not having a yard can be a dealbreaker when choosing a property, but it doesn't have to be. Small outdoor spaces shouldn't hamper your desire to garden, whether it's purely for enjoyment, for aesthetics or to be more self-sufficient. And with our busy schedules, it makes more sense to have a smaller garden. Your small garden will be manageable and not overwhelming—fun rather than a burden.

The want and need to garden has not changed. In fact, around the world it has either kept pace with former generations or grown leaps and bounds in young demographics. This growth shouldn't be a surprise, what with the threats to food security, pollution, food prices and a human need to remain connected to the earth and to nature in some form or other. As our lives get busier and our outdoor spaces get smaller, we tend to crave the time and means to take things down a notch, relax, contemplate and reconnect, and I can't think of a better way to do so than to spend time gardening. And the reality is that there is nothing that can stop you.

I live in an apartment-style condominium, with only a balcony on which to garden. I also share the gardens at my childhood home where my parents still

Making space for nature is important in the sterile environment of a city.

live today, and from time to time I rent a plot in a community garden or help out in a friend's garden so that I can increase my yields. There are so many ways to grow plants even when you have minimal space in which to do it, and I'm going to show you how.

The bottom line is that a garden isn't what it used to be. Gardens can be grown *anywhere*. Just because you're only able to accommodate one container to grow lettuce doesn't mean you aren't a gardener or that you do not have a garden. You are a gardener, and your one pot of lettuce is your garden. Gardening has evolved—sometimes you have to think, or garden, outside the box.

Why Bother?

These days, any outdoor space, particularly in an urban environment, is an invaluable space. We pay a premium price for property, regardless of size, and we can't afford to waste those precious spaces. Certainly people are still buying and developing large properties with big yards, but ironically those outdoor spaces are frequently left as a plot of grass, used only recreationally or not at all. Too many people think it's either too expensive or too hard to landscape or garden. It's not difficult to find these forgotten and neglected yards; I suspect you can think of a few you pass by every day on your way to work. Often these spaces are filled with good intentions, and sometimes they do come to fruition with beautiful landscaping, but rarely do they have anything to harvest for the kitchen table throughout the season. There was never a more important opportunity to use the spaces we have, however small, to reconnect with our food sources, and if nothing else, just to get your hands dirty and experience something that can provide you and your family with a fun and truly fulfilling experience.

It's almost impossible to be completely self-sufficient in the city; it's difficult even if you own and operate a farm-like setting. Our climate from coast to coast to coast simply does not allow for us to rely completely on what we can grow at home, but we can supplement our regular intake of grocery store produce in a wide variety of ways and on varied levels.

For example, you can grow your own herbs. Certainly herbs don't offer much in the way of sustenance, but growing them saves money because you don't have to purchase them from a store, and it doesn't require very much time and energy from a busy schedule. And the result offers organic, natural ways to flavour your food and maybe even improve your health if the herbs have any medicinal qualities to offer. Many herbs can be grown on your windowsill indoors if you don't have an outdoor space to work with. Even a few vegetables can be grown indoors, without a greenhouse, with little effort.

It's important to grow things in the sterile environment of concrete that makes up a city. City gardens, though relatively small, tend to be more biologically diverse than most rural gardens and farmland. Urban gardens draw

Growing herbs on your balcony is easy.

wildlife back to the city, to hardscapes where there was no previous reason for birds, insects and small mammals to visit or live. These gardens act as wildlife corridors, allowing for a wide range of wildlife to move from one garden to another, providing diverse habitats for those animals.

In this modern world, despite all of our technological advances, biodiversity is what keeps us alive. Without pollinating insects, particularly bees, we would not survive. Making space for nature, no matter how small, is important not only to us but also to every other living creature. We all rely upon one another. We tend to forget that green spaces provide us with oxygen and help to cool our cities. Green spaces also provide foodstuffs for those wild creatures, as well as places where they can live and breed, a sort of protection or preservation of varied species. When we remain in touch with nature through gardening, particularly in an urban setting, every creature connected to the natural world, including our species, benefits.

This all being said, stick around, open your mind to the possibilities of gardening and be willing to experiment. I will provide you with the information and tools necessary to plan, grow and harvest, in the smallest of spaces to the slightly more expansive ones, with organic gardening methods for the best results. And it's worth mentioning that I will focus more on growing plants that will provide you with something in the way of foodstuffs rather than growing plants strictly for their beauty. Food security is critical these days, and I hope to encourage every city dweller to grow as much of their own food as they can— believe me, you'll thank me later. But the rest is up to you, and the only thing you need is a little imagination and the willingness to get a little dirty.

Green spaces attract wildlife, provide us with oxygen and help to cool our cities.

Finding a Garden Space

If you have a deck, yard or balcony—or even if you don't—you have space to garden. It doesn't take much, so don't feel discouraged. Take a look around. Is there an alleyway with a good amount of sun? Is there a grassy meridian between the public sidewalk and the street? If so, would you be allowed to plant up a few containers or raised beds along the alleyway or meridian?

What about a stairwell or a fence? Vertical spaces are often overlooked and neglected when it comes to gardening. They can accommodate and support climbing plants, particularly vegetable plants such as peas and beans, and the container at the base can be quite narrow so that it doesn't become an obstruction or safety hazard.

Is there a communal space shared with your neighbours? If so, can you obtain permission to grow plants there for all to enjoy? There are bound to be neighbours who will pitch in. Perhaps beds already exist strictly for ornamentals in your condo or townhouse community; maybe you can help plant them up and in exchange add some vegetable and fruit plants to the mix. Edibles can be just as attractive as any annual, and they will produce food for you and your neighbours.

If all you have is a tiny space, you can still grow plants in tiny containers.

Use your imagination, and remember that you're not restricted to your own personal space, especially if it turns out that you don't have any outdoors at all. If you want to garden in urban settings, there is a plethora of options for you, but you may have to venture out of your humble abode.

Finding Space at Home

Most people who live in the city have some form of outdoor space that belongs to them, whether it's a tiny townhouse yard or a balcony attached to their apartment or condominium. If you have such a space, small or not the gardening possibilities are endless. However, even if you don't have any outdoor space of your own, or you just want more space, you can grow plants in a variety of shared spaces throughout a property—with permission of course. These spaces are often in great abundance but are frequently ignored, neglected and overlooked, and you may have to use your imagination and a little creativity to see their potential. Once you obtain permission from management, strata councils

Find ways to make use of any available space at home.

and condominium boards and spread the word throughout the building or complex, you might just find that other residents had the same idea, spurring on a small movement of people who all want to grow plants close to home.

Common Spaces

Many multi-dwelling buildings have common spaces, and these are available and open to all residents within the building. You usually pay fees, either separately in condo or strata fees, or as part of your rent, so you may as well use the space. Often there is an outdoor space with a patio, a courtyard or a rooftop to share with your neighbours, and these are ideal spaces in which to garden, whether you do so individually or collectively.

Getting started will take some planning because each space in each building will be slightly different in layout and usage, but the first step should always be to ask for permission from the management company that maintains the building's common spaces, or the condo or strata board, or both, before going ahead with your garden. There have been cases of people who have gone ahead with a garden project without permission, and the result wasn't positive to say the least. Even if a project is done for all the right reasons, without the necessary approval it may become a prickly subject, and in some cases can even result in fines. It's better to be safe than sorry.

Obtaining the approval to begin gardening in your building's common spaces may require more than just an

Common spaces are ideal spaces in which to garden.

There is plenty of garden space in this common front yard for all of the residents.

informal question posed to the powers that be. In some cases, you may need to draw up a formal proposal. If you do find yourself in that situation, there are several things to consider. Even if your building's management doesn't require a formal proposal, it doesn't hurt to have a plan.

First you have to decide whether you want to go on with the proposal alone or with your neighbours as a group. I suspect that there are others in the building who are feeling similarly to you and want the same thing but either didn't know where to start or were too bashful to approach anyone about it. Is the space large enough to share with others, and are you able to donate the time necessary to properly set up and take care of the area throughout the growing season? As enjoyable as gardening is, it can be a lot of work, and that work is much more fun when shared with others.

Put up an informative poster in an approved common area notifying your neighbours of your intentions, and see who replies with interest. If there is more than one person who wants to take the project on with you, you'll have the advantage of numbers. The board or strata council and management company may be more likely to consider a group proposal than an individual one, and having a group takes some of the pressure off and lessens the workload. And you get to meet your neighbours and interact with them when you might not have done so otherwise.

Being prepared for the proposal, regardless of the level of formality, is critical. Things to consider for the proposal are very similar to what you'd have to consider if you had your own balcony or deck on which to garden. Have something specific in mind before approaching the management company or board of directors.

Survey the area in advance and make a plan of what you'd like to grow where, and possibly with who. Just as you would with your own space, you need to evaluate what the space has to offer and what it needs to best determine what types of plants will grow there. Whether you want to grow vegetables, ornamentals or a combination of the two, success will depend on the amount of sun, exposure and so on (see pages 45–54 for greater detail on evaluating your garden space).

Other practical considerations include the flooring surface. If your potential garden space is ground level and the surface is concrete, then you should have no problem with the weight of containers, but if you're wanting to use an old wooden deck, it may have trouble supporting heavy containers or raised beds. Where is the water source? Is there one, and at what distance is it from the actual space? Will you require a hose to water the garden, or will you be hauling buckets from inside the building? Maybe you can even set up a water collection system from the building itself, such as a few rain barrels. Whatever your situation may be, it's much better to determine the elements critical for your success now rather than later.

One other important step to putting together a proposal is to work out a list of necessary supplies and the cost for those supplies. This list will be your opportunity to find out who will pay for such a project. If you're providing

the labour, then maybe the board will foot the bill for the supplies, or a portion thereof.

Sometimes groups will come together to create revenue within the building for projects just like this one. In my condominium, residents came up with the idea

Evaluate your space and plan what to plant in it accordingly—for example, sunflowers need lots of sun.

A courtyard is the perfect place to build attractive raised beds.

to start a recycle operation in the underground parkade, where anyone in the building could bring their bottles and cans to the secure area for the volunteers to take to the depot. The money raised from the returnables has created enough of a fund that we've been able to buy the plants for the garden beds, as well as purchase park benches to place throughout the property, with some left over for other things for our amenity room.

Not every building will have such a fund to draw from, but there could be some unused money in the budget that could go toward what is needed. If not, then a compromise may have to be reached; you may have to start with fewer supplies, or chip in for them yourself. Tell the group you're asking permission from that you and any other residents involved are committed to the project

for a minimum of one year. Prior to the end of the year's commitment, they can come to you to confirm if you'll be committing to another year, and with who, so they're not left all of a sudden with the materials they have purchased and no one to use them. A lack of commitment can be a deal breaker for such a proposal.

Keep in mind that proposals of this nature, being that the end result is not critical to the day-to-day operations of a building, may take some time to come to fruition on the part of those who are making the decisions. It may take six months to a year for the proposal to be addressed, budgeted and approved. As with most forms of democracy, sometimes the wheels turn very slowly, and it's important to know this ahead of time. Just because you are raring to get going doesn't mean that they will be. Sometimes, the more detailed and specific the proposal, the better the result, but it all depends on the situation at hand.

If all goes well, and you're given permission to go ahead, you might want to consider, if you've developed the plan and the space with others, what their availability is so that the garden's needs are met regularly. An informal schedule might be necessary at first, but once everyone falls into their niche, the schedule becomes more relaxed, and everyone knows their role and what is needed. Most importantly, have fun with the space, and know that your hard work will be enjoyed by so many people for years to come.

Corridors and Stairways

Corridors of any kind are often overlooked. Granted the surrounding structures can cause corridors to be shady places, but shade does not leave one without plants to grow—quite the opposite. If your corridor receives less than six hours a day of good sunlight, then all you have to do is choose plants that prefer shade. If the area receives six or more hours of good sunlight, then sun-loving plants are best, including most vegetable and fruit plants. As long as there is enough of a footpath available then you can begin to plant the space accordingly, and depending on the width of the corridor, you may even be able to plant in the middle as well as along the sides, creating two footpaths rather than only one.

Stairways are often neglected spaces as well. As long as there is ample room, both for people to move freely and safely up and down the staircase and for plants to grow, most any stairway can be used as a garden space. Ideally, custom-made planters are fixed to the bottom of the railing and planted with vines, which can grow upward to maximize the space.

Corridors are often overlooked but make great garden spaces.

Food-producing crops such as beans and peas are perfect, provided they have enough light.

If the corridor or stairway you want to use is in a common area, be sure to get permission from your apartment manager, strata council or condo board association before planting anything. You don't want your garden to come down for bylaw infractions.

Rooftop Gardening

Rooftop gardening is one of the latest trends in the horticultural arena and is growing in popularity around the country. Rooftop gardens come in different forms, from a thick layer of soil over an impermeable membrane that covers most of the roof surface to a simple collection of containers set on the roof.

There are many advantages to rooftop gardening. Rooftop gardens extend the growing season, as rooftops tend to be a warmer and drier microclimate. Rooftop container gardens reduce pest problems even further than containers set on the ground because any pest that has to crawl or walk to find its host, from a slug to a browsing deer, is out of luck. Vandalism and theft are practically eliminated as well. Rooftop gardens in large urban centres provide respite for birds and butterflies that might otherwise lack adequate food and shelter.

Container gardening is ideal for a rooftop setting, but you must make sure the roof is sturdy enough to handle the weight of the pots, plants, soil and water. Hire a structural engineer to determine how much weight your roof can hold. You may be able to have your containers on the roof in spring, summer and fall but need to remove them for winter if you get any appreciable snow

The simplest way to garden on a rooftop is in containers.

cover; the roof might not take the weight of the containers and snow combined.

You will need to have a handy source of water for watering the plants. There will be more sunlight and wind on the rooftop than at ground level, and containers will need to be watered frequently, possibly every day. Consider incorporating water-holding polymers into the potting soil, and use mulch to reduce evaporation and keep the soil moist for longer periods. It is a good idea to trap as much rainwater for use as possible. You do not want to be hauling buckets of water up to the roof to water plants if there is no available water source such as a tap and hose. Pots, plants, soil and other supplies will also need to be transported to the rooftop.

Plants will be more exposed to sun and wind on a roof than at ground level.

Winds at rooftop level can be strong enough to break trees and shred herbaceous plants. Sturdy windbreaks protect the plants from strong winds. Windbreaks will also provide some shade from intense afternoon sun and some privacy from the neighbours if their building is taller than yours. Evergreen plants in containers need extra protection in winter, as the wind and sun can quickly desicate a plant. Some plants may be better adapted to rooftop culture than others. Heat-loving, drought-tolerant plants, such as hens and chicks, are the best choices for a rooftop garden setting.

If you've been given the go-ahead by both the engineer and your condo board or landlord, there are simple ways of going about creating a rooftop garden. Both new and recycled elements can be used, and maybe with some help from your neighbours, you can turn your rooftop into a beautiful and practical space for people to reconnect to nature. If there is room, you might even want to add a place to sit, maybe a bench or a table and chairs. Just remember that a rooftop garden doesn't need to be complicated, fussy or professionally designed to be very much appreciated.

Vertical Gardening

When you're looking for garden spaces, don't forget to think vertically. Vertical gardening is one of the most popular types of growing in small spaces—and for good reason. Vertical gardening is a method of gardening where plants are grown upward rather than outward. It makes use of vertical space, such as walls, that would otherwise remain empty. Thankfully people have been coming up with new and interesting ways to garden on walls and even in the air, and I imagine that the options will only increase over time. It's simple: often there is no other way to grow but up!

Vertical gardens can be used to block an ugly view or provide privacy. In small urban spaces, vertical gardens are most often used to maximize available space for efficient usage and accessibility. Vertical gardening also allows the disabled and elderly easier access for maintaining the plants and enjoying the garden.

Vines are perfect for vertical gardening.

Vertical gardening is easy to do in containers. One of the most common methods is to set a container below some sort of climbing structure. Plants can be trained to grow up trellises, fences, arbours, pergolas and walls. Vines and other natural climbers are great choices for growing on trellises and other structures. Some vines will naturally twine around a structure, some will attach themselves to the structure with tendrils, aerial rootlets or suction cups, and some will need to be attached to the structure with soft ties. You will need to ensure that the container and climbing structure are sturdy enough to handle the weight of the plant without tipping over, and that they will not blow over in a strong wind.

Hanging baskets make use of air space. Plants can be grown in hanging baskets and allowed to trail and spill over the edge of the basket. Hanging baskets can be hung from any sturdy support, including the undersides of upper balconies, beams and commercially available poles affixed to balcony edges and railings.

Plants can also be grown in a variety of specialized containers, including multiple-opening containers, stackable containers and grow walls. We are all familiar with the terracotta strawberry planter that has large openings in which to plant. There are now many different styles of commercially available containers with multiple openings. Stackable containers allow for more plants to be grown in a small surface area than do regular containers or garden beds. Grow walls are containers that have a vertical planting surface. One type of grow wall is a tall, flat, upright container that resembles a section of lattice fence with plants poking out. A grow wall can stand alone or be incorporated as part of a building wall. If custom made, the wall unit can be designed with your style in mind, whether it be contemporary, modern, traditional or classic.

Some pest problems experienced in more traditional garden settings are reduced or eliminated in a containerized vertical garden. Hanging baskets prevent crawling pests from reaching plants. Also, the plants are more exposed to air,

Hanging baskets make use of air space.

which reduces the incidence of many different diseases.

Your vertical container garden requires the same type of maintenance as a regular container garden, except that the plants may need to be watered more frequently. A layer of mulch will help to retain moisture. There are a few other points to keep in mind when planning your vertical container garden. Try to grow plants that will remain in easy reach for maintenance. If you are growing sun-loving plants, place the climbing structure on the north side of the plants. Do the reverse for shade-loving plants. Also, be aware of the direction of the prevailing wind, and face the plants into the wind so that the wind pushes the plants onto the structure.

Finding Space Farther from Home

In situations where there is no place to garden on your own home turf, or if you simply want more space than you have at home, you will have to go a little farther away from your back door. There are many different means of gardening outside of your home. Some are new while others have been around since the beginning of time.

Living in the city can be a cold experience if you let it be. Community in many ways has been lost, but gardening outside of your home, in a variety of ways, even for selfish reasons, is a way of rebuilding that sense of community. Often we end up connecting with others when all we wanted to do was garden; I think it's in gardeners' natures to connect with one another, just like our wanting to be connected to the soil and the plants. Whether you garden on your balcony or in a community garden, you'll find yourself connecting with others in ways you never thought possible and having heaps of fun. It never ceases to amaze me how interconnected and interesting the gardening community is.

Gardening outside of your home is a great way to connect with the gardening community.

Community Gardens

Community gardens are not a new concept but are often overlooked. They are a great alternative for anyone looking for a space, or more space, in which to garden, and you can grow anything you want in a community plot. Maybe your balcony has only three hours of sunlight daily, which eliminates some of the things you've been desperately wanting to grow. You could always rent a sunny plot in a community garden. It's often the case that community gardens are located in very exposed locations, so there is no shortage of sunny plots to be had. Or maybe you've just always wanted to try to grow annuals—beautiful, flowering, prolific annuals—but you can't at home. Then community gardens are for you. Usually the only contribution needed, aside from a small fee, is to help out a bit throughout the season with general maintenance.

There are many benefits to supporting or taking part in a community garden. It's a place to learn if you're interested in doing so. Certainly you can be left to your own devices, but a community garden is a place where people can field questions back and forth and learn from each other's mistakes and successes. Meeting new people who share your desire to garden can lead to friendships you may never have had otherwise. This is the "community" in "community garden."

There are some disadvantages to garden plots in community gardens, such as high demand. Often plots are in short supply. Find out where your community gardens are and what is available. You may have to wait out a season, but it would be worth it in the end. Proximity can also be a problem. Sometimes, if you want to garden badly enough, and the only plots available are far away, you may have to travel some. Depending on how secure the garden is, you may experience

Community gardens are one solution for urban gardeners who are short on space.

theft or vandalism. I would consider this rare, but it can happen, and it's something to keep in mind but certainly nothing to be discouraged about.

Community gardens are springing up everywhere, even in the smallest of municipalities. You may walk or drive by them on a daily basis without even knowing that they're there. They can range in size from only a few plots to huge projects that encompass hundreds of plots. Quite often they're located in temporary locations such as empty lots in urban centres, but they are becoming more and more common in permanent locations beside schools, universities, parks and community league shared spaces. Community gardens are as diverse as those who garden in them.

In a nutshell, a community garden is a plot of land where people from the community come to garden. The plot of land is divided up into sections that are assigned to individuals, or families, to grow vegetables, fruit, herbs or sometimes simply flowering plants to beautify the area. Usually there is a fee attached to the section one receives for the season. The fee is extremely reasonable and covers the space you'll be using as well as any water that may be available.

There are a few ways to determine what the best community garden is for you. Friends and neighbours are great resources for information. Even if they haven't used any space in the garden they're recommending, they likely know it from the neighbourhood, or from friends of theirs who have used the space. Another resource is your city's website. Often the city has some involvement with community gardens and will have a section on its website listing what they're called, where they're located and any other necessary information, such as contact numbers.

As well, community gardens are usually connected through their own network

Community gardens are as diverse as those who garden in them.

of sorts. This is the case in Edmonton. Formerly known as the Community Garden Network (CGN), the newly named Sustainable Food Edmonton has absorbed a number of entities that encompass similar mandates: accessibility to gardening, food security and community. The following is a quote from a CGN member about the benefits of community gardening in Edmonton: "In 2001, more than 835 families increased their consumption of fresh, organic fruits and vegetables by growing their own food in community gardens. In 2002 and 2003, over 100 youth and children accessed programming hosted at three community gardens: growing their own food, caring for plants, and observing wildlife. On average, a community garden plot grows about $100 worth of fresh produce each year, which makes for an approximate $287,000 contribution to food self reliance in the City." These statistics are huge and prove how important these spaces are to any municipality. It's no surprise that they're becoming more and more popular.

Unfortunately, there isn't a central group or website to go to for information on communtity gardens from coast to coast. If you can't find what you need on your city's website, you may have to connect with someone in your local horticultural society for information on community garden groups. Or go to your local library for help finding community gardens close to home and right for your needs.

Not every community garden will be part of an organized network, but the basis of any shared space will be passion for gardening, and that's reason enough to get involved. The types of gardens can vary, however. Often the garden is designed with the community's needs in mind. Some may be to beautify an area while others are more open to whatever you want to grow.

Usually the amount of involvement you want to contribute is all you'll be asked to do, but prior to actually leasing a space for the growing season, it's important to identify whether you're only required to tend the plot you've been given or if the garden overall is more communal in nature. The type of garden you choose to participate in should reflect what you are comfortable contributing, what time you have to commit and what your goals are. Are you short on time and only wanting to grow some

Take the time to find the right community garden for you.

vegetables to supplement your own supply, or are you more interested in getting involved in the community as a whole by committing more of your time and efforts to the project? It's something you need to ask yourself honestly. If community gardening is new to you, and you're unsure, then I recommend starting small and possibly sticking to your own plot, if this is an option. If you already have a clear goal of getting your hands dirty and pitching in wherever necessary, then go for it. Remember, it only has to be for one season. If you decide you want to increase or decrease your level of involvement, then keep that in mind for the following season.

Beyond the time and labour commitments you're willing to make, getting involved in a community garden and deciding what and how much to grow can come down to what is available in the garden, such as water. Water sources can range from collected rainfall in barrels to a common tap and hose to water brought in from other locations. Depending on how new the garden space is, what type of funding, if any, it has, its proximity to the plumbing necessary to have a hose on site, and how big the actual garden is, water may be scarce. It's important to select plants based on their water requirements, just as you would choose based on sunlight and space needs. If you choose plants with extremely high water needs and there is no water source on site, you'll quickly find yourself regretting your choices.

Once you've made the decision to get involved in a community garden, the most important thing to do is to have fun with the space. The first season using a plot within a community garden will lead to future seasons if you're willing to experiment, evaluate and monitor what takes place throughout the season and what you would do differently. There is no such thing as failure, only new experiences and lessons in how to make your community garden a resounding success.

A handy water source is a definite plus in a community garden.

Gardening at School or Work

Another option is sharing spaces to garden at school or work. This concept may be new, but it is becoming more and more popular. Perhaps your workplace has an outdoor space such as a deck or patio for the staff that is sunny and has an accessible water source. All you need is an open-minded employer who is willing to let you do the work, but probably with a few guarantees—after all, you still have to do your job.

I have two friends who garden at school and work, respectively. One friend gardens at the college she attends. Her faculty has a student area cordoned off to anyone outside of that faculty. She grows a combination of herbs and vegetables throughout the growing season, not only for herself but for her classmates as well. The agreement is that if her classmates use what's growing in the containers, they have to help out a bit with the watering, sowing successive crops and a bit of pinching when necessary, and it works out beautifully. It took a couple of years to get it down to a workable system, but now her school garden provides some of her fresh produce for up to six months of the year. As most people have experienced, those school days can be very long, weeks blending into years, and being on a student's budget during that time is tough, so the supplemental vegetables and herbs are not only convenient, fresh, delicious and plentiful but also inexpensive.

Another friend took over the decorative planters at his office. He too has an agreement that anyone who wants to partake in the produce must help out with the maintenance, but he's really the only one who takes advantage of the garden space. Gardening at work allows him to satisfy his need to grow because he simply doesn't have even a stitch of outdoor space of his own.

Consider growing vegetables and herbs at school or work.

Urban Farming

My parents still live in the house I was raised in. They aren't ready to move on, but as they age, they no longer want to garden—or can, quite honestly, with various injuries and declining physical ability. Over the years I've built a number of beds, not only to up the curb appeal but also to make a beautiful space for my parents to enjoy, even if they can't do the gardening themselves. Using their yard allows me to garden like a madwoman without the steep property taxes.

I have a number of friends who also use available space in their friends' gardens, and other friends who are urban farmers. Urban farmers find people in their community who have unused garden plots. Either they rent the space for a small fee or they're allowed to use it freely but give the owners some of the produce that is harvested. This arrangement usually works out perfectly, both for the person in the home who's unable to use the space and for the one willing to use it, do the work and share the results.

Urban farming encompasses a variety of great methods to use existing garden spaces that are not already being used, quite often the gardens that belong to private homes. As people grow older, or busier, they may no longer be able to use the garden space on their property. It's pretty rare that the space is converted into something else. The garden just reverts to a weed bed and is wasted.

An urban farming movement, started years ago, gave momentum to and motivated people who wanted to farm in an urban environment using existing plots in residential neighbourhoods. Certainly you don't have to become a large-scale urban farmer. You can, however, use the same methodology to create a win-win situation for you and someone in your neighbourhood.

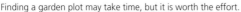
Finding a garden plot may take time, but it is worth the effort.

The search for a potential gardening plot may take some time, but finally finding the perfect garden and striking a deal with the owner is worth the effort. If there is a home in your neighbourhood that has an unused vegetable garden plot, consider either approaching the homeowners directly or leaving a detailed letter in their mailbox, including contact information, regarding a proposal to use their garden plot to grow vegetables and possibly some flowers. A deal can be struck where you promise that you will be the grower and caretaker of the plot throughout the season, including clean-up at the end, and for letting you use the plot, the owner will receive a percentage of the produce harvested. This way, the homeowner reaps the benefits from the garden's harvest, as do you, and the space is used and cared for rather than being neglected and wasted. If the homeowner wants to participate in some way, incorporate that and any other details in the contract necessary to make it work for everyone involved. You could also offer to pay a fee for the use of the garden, just as you would pay a fee for a community garden plot. It's one of many ways to make the partnership benefit both sides involved in the urban farming initiative.

The beauty of this kind of arrangement is that it can be done totally on your own, but it can also be part of a growing network of urban farming initiatives. Kitsilano Farms in Vancouver, BC, has created an urban farm network of residential garden spaces in the Kitsilano neighbourhood and throughout the west side of Vancouver that are available for people to garden, rather than letting the gardens go unused. This particular network stipulates that the spaces provided be used to grow organic produce that is then sold at markets throughout the city. However, a similar network could be created wherein the growers decide for themselves how to distribute the produce, donating any surplus to friends, family or the food bank. In fact, you might want to grow a row or two specifically with the intent to donate the produce to the food bank in support of the national initiative known as *Plant a Row • Grow a Row*, a people-helping-people program to assist in feeding the hungry in your community.

Both you and the homeowner can enjoy the harvest.

Guerilla Gardening

If you're a little bit too rebellious to want to be part of an organized urban farming network, then guerilla gardening might be for you. In some ways, it can be similar to the method of obtaining permission from an individual in your neighbourhood to garden on their property—except for the obtaining permission part. There are varied levels of guerilla gardening, from planting some flowers in your neighbour's garden as a gesture of goodwill to making seed bombs and releasing them into public spaces, such as grassy meridians or abandoned lots, to grow and thrive.

Guerilla gardening is for anyone with rebellious soul and a green thumb.

Guerilla gardening is nothing new. The basis of this practice is taking gardening to the streets. Many guerilla gardeners get involved to plant up a space with flowers or edibles for strangers to enjoy, but often with the intention of never returning to the space to maintain the plants. In this way a person is able to satisfy a need to grow things, and at the same time contribute to their community in some small, yet anonymous and somewhat sneaky way.

Seed bombs are made up of compressed soil and a mix of flower or vegetable seeds, to be tossed into spaces where they will eventually break down and germinate. Never plant or seed anything that is invasive or noxious because you likely will never be back to tend the plants, and if they get out of hand, it's not fair for anyone in that space to be left with the mess.

In no way do I condone guerilla gardening in a destructive, harmful or disrespectful way, and certainly not in any way that breaks any laws. Guerilla gardening is a somewhat covert operation, hence the reference to guerilla, but it should always be done in a respectful, positive, beneficial and ecologically sustainable way. There is always the risk that you might get caught, so being respectful and cautious is key. If you do get caught, whoever catches you should want to say, "Thank you."

A wide variety of material now exists online for would-be guerilla gardeners, with tips, hints and recipes to satisfy your rebellious gardening soul.

Optimizing Your Garden Space

It's time to make the next move. A space has been determined, and now it is time to find inspiration, while focusing on your needs and wants, for your urban garden. By evaluating the space you've chosen, you'll then be able to determine what will be best for growing in that location. Will containers fit the bill? Is there room for a raised bed or two? And if so, will it be filled with nutritious, organic edible plants or bursting with colourful shrubs and perennials? The following information can be used as guidelines to follow for optimizing your garden space.

Ideas and Inspiration

People who garden in small spaces sometimes have to use innovative, even ingenious ways to make the most of the space they have with maximum efficiency and accessibility. There is a myriad of ways to do this.

You don't have to look far for inspiration. You only have to look at the space itself. Often it will dictate what it really needs to be efficiently maximized. There are questions you can ask yourself; for example, if you have a balcony, figure out

Look around you and get inspired; even a small balcony can become a lush garden.

its potential by asking the following. Is the space incredibly narrow? Is the balcony big enough for containers and a footpath? Is there a balcony or ceiling of some kind above your balcony? If so, is it capable of having something hanging from it, such as a single hanging basket or a hanging vertical garden assembly? Is the wall surface in the space capable of supporting a vertical or wall planter of some kind? Is the railing on the balcony capable of holding planters, and if so, would they be best placed on top of the railing or on the walls of the railing?

Those are only a few of the questions necessary to spark an idea storm. I hope to inspire you even further with some conventional ideas and some eclectic ones. If you want to see more ideas, my best advice would be to search through other reference materials at the library, bookstores and on the web. There are people

around the globe who are blowing my mind with their ideas for small urban spaces, and gardens continue to pop up in the most unlikely of places. Even a stroll through your community can be inspiring. Take a look at what your neighbours are doing in their spaces; possibly they have ingenious creations of their own never done anywhere else, ideas you can repeat in your space.

The following sections are a breakdown of suggestions and ideas based on the method or container used: containers for balcony/deck railings, windowsills and fences, hanging and upside-down planters, vertical planters, wall-mounted systems, pillar and column gardens, shelving, standard and tiered raised beds, fold-away and collapsible planters, ready-to-assemble kits, and recycled containers and other eclectic innovations.

A succulent garden doesn't need much space, as this innovative container proves.

Railing planters give this building a cheerful appearance.

Containers for Railings, Windowsills and Fences

Any balcony has a railing, and many decks do too. Railings have been well used over the years but could be used even more, and in different ways. There is a wide variety of planters available just for this purpose, made with safety, durability and stability in mind. Purchasing one might be better than building one yourself; it's not impossible for a railing planter to fall if not installed properly or built from a poor design, and it's not worth someone getting hurt to save a few bucks. Railing planters come in just about every colour, style and material you could imagine. They're also available in self-watering models.

Windowsills and window boxes have been used seemingly forever, but they have decreased in usage somewhat over the years—maybe because the older, traditional look has become tired and outdated. There was little in the way of choice in the past, but things have changed, and as with any other type of container, there are lots of materials, colours, styles and sizes to choose from. More importantly, window boxes are an ideal solution for people with little in the way of space in which to garden. Everyone has windows.

Window boxes don't have to be boring.

Fences are too often overlooked as a garden space. They are vertical, ideal for growing up rather than out. I use the chainlink fence surrounding my parents' garden for growing things such as kiwi and grape vines vertically, it supports our raspberry bush row, and I can also grow peas and beans on it in summer. The only thing you have to consider really is the style of fence and the styles of containers and/or types of plants it will support. From that point, the only limit is your imagination.

Hanging and Upside-down Gardens

These gardening methods sound self-explanatory, but they can be expanded on a very simple goal: growing plants in a supported and suspended container, either from the top or bottom surfaces.

Over the past few years, there has been a kitschy, but useful, planter system on the market known by a variety of names, and I suspect you will recognize it. It basically offers you the opportunity to grow individual or multiple plants in one hanging system. The most popular of the bunch is the Topsy-Turvy system. There are different styles, depending on what you want to grow—tomatoes, other vegetables such as peppers, herbs, strawberries— and even one that will attract hummingbirds. They're all readily available and inexpensive, easy to plant and maintain and really work well. Any hanging planter, whatever the style, is great because it saves floor space that could otherwise be used for other containers or for walking space. It's basically a space maximizer.

The Topsy-Turvy planters can be used as inspiration to make your own upside-down garden for little cost and effort. Often the supplies needed are already around the house or easy to obtain from friends and family for free, and you can customize the planters as you see fit. They're maybe not as pleasing to the eye, but beauty is in the eye of the beholder, and I think the more

Upside-down containers are a great way to grow tomatoes.

Strawberries grow well in hanging multi-opening containers.

creative the urban gardeners, the more stunning the ideas tend to be. Five-gallon buckets are perfect for home-made upside-down planters. The handle is already built-in for hanging, and the plastic is easy to puncture, cut and drill for assembly. They can also be set up with a self-watering system to reduce the need for carrying out a watering can (see page 64 for how).

As with anything that is suspended, it's essential to determine if it can be hung safely from an appropriate support. If you're wanting to hang it from the ceiling of a balcony above your own, for example, find out if your upstairs neighbours are also gardening on their balcony. They may have already pushed the boundaries of weight on their own, and a heavy garden suspended underneath may be the tipping point. Certainly one hanging basket won't take a balcony down, but a heavy suspended system

might, depending on the structural integrity of the support. The weight of the system itself must be accounted for, along with the potting medium, plants and water.

Vertical Planters

Vertical planters cover quite a bit of territory. A vertical planter can be suspended, such as the upside-down containers, or they can be fixed to a wall, hung on a wall independent from a unifying structure, or simply placed against a wall, but not necessarily for support. Vertical gardening systems, or planters, can be stacked or layered for maximum efficiency or used as a single unit, with one or several plants sharing the potting medium.

Stackable, multi-opening containers make use of vertical space.

Make sure your wall or fence can support the weight of the containers you're hanging on it.

Wall-mounted systems are one way to grow up rather than out. You can make your own, or they are commercially available. All of these systems need a wall, fence or other vertical support strong enough to hold the weight of both container and plants. As with other systems, as long as the drainage is adequate and there is room for the roots of the plants, then you're good to go. Wall-mounted systems can vary dramatically in price, and if budget is a concern, then homemade is the way to go.

Pillar and column systems are another way to garden vertically, but these methods are fixed, free-standing and in a recognizable pillar or column shape. With a little skill, one could build one of these systems from scratch with the space in mind, but there are kits available as well, and they are usually easy to assemble and maintain. They're also easy to water because of the tubing from top to bottom in the centre of the planter that allows water to saturate all of the potting mix, rather than just soaking the top and leaving the bottom bone dry. Pillar systems are great for any small space, and they can range in size from only a few feet tall to heights that would require a ladder to water. The only thing to keep in mind with such a system is that it will need access to light on all sides for even growth, or as an alternative, it will need to be rotated on a regular basis.

It's funny how most people don't often think of using simple shelving systems on their balconies and patios. They're ideal for maximizing available space by placing containers on the shelves that go up rather than out, and they're easy to access for any type of maintenance, particularly watering. The most important factor to consider when choosing a shelving system is how much weight it can hold. The shelf materials are a factor. Wood is okay, but the shelves, legs and supports all have to be thick enough and strong enough to withstand the weight of the planters, particularly when wet, and they need to be able to tolerate the harsh conditions of an outdoor environment. Outdoor shelves are available in most hardware stores and are quite economical. They may be the best choice for this type of application simply because they were designed to withstand the elements, and often weighty items as well. Otherwise, wooden shelves, if strong enough, can be stained or varnished for their longevity, and most shelves can be reinforced with brackets for little cost.

Standard and Tiered Raised Beds

Most people are familiar with raised beds, even tiered raised beds, but they too have come a long way over the years. Not only can they be used in a conventional way in a traditional garden setting, such as in a yard, big or small, but they can also be used on balconies, decks, patios and any other flat surface. A few of the styles may require some type of support, such as a wall to lean up against. Weight may be an issue as well, as raised beds can get quite large, and therefore heavy, but they are incredibly easy to maintain. You can construct your own raised beds, or you can buy them in prefabricated kit form. The options are endless (see pages 67–77 for more on raised beds).

There are ready-to-assemble kits galore to choose from in the gardening marketplace, whether from your local garden centre, a garden supply website or a mail-order catalogue. They range greatly in price, but often that price includes the convenience of not having to put any thought into the design or construction, only the assembly. Kits are ideal for those who aren't handy, don't have the time to source out materials or to construct something from scratch, and just don't want to mess around with anything other than a bit of assembly. There

Tiered raised beds are both visually appealing and practical.

are kits for just about every size and style of raised bed, particularly ingenious designs for those who garden in small spaces because there's been such a demand for ways to garden on a smaller scale in the past few years.

Collapsible Containers

Fold-away and collapsible planters are probably the newest option, and are most inspirational of all because they are the perfect solution for the apartment or condo dweller. These types of containers are soft sided and collapse nearly flat, so they are ideal for storage when not in use over winter. They're incredibly sturdy, practical, reasonably priced and readily available on the market, clearly because there is a huge demand for such a product.

This collapsible potato planter comes with a handy pocket for harvesting.

Recycled Containers and Other Eclectic Innovations

A recycled container can really be anything that had a previous use but is no longer needed for that purpose. The only limit is your imagination. As long as there is adequate drainage and room for roots, almost anything can be used.

Materials designed for other purposes, such as piping, eaves troughs and plastic pop bottles or milk jugs, are ideal for this method of gardening, as are other household items. Burlap or heavy-duty fabric sacks allow for a deep, soft-sided container ideal for planting on the side as well as on top. Hang an old handbag from the banister of a balcony or deck for a bit of whimsy, or drill some holes in the bottom of an old metal watering can for drainage and plant it up. In larger settings, such as a townhouse backyard, I have seen old claw-foot bathtubs used as a raised bed of sorts. Nothing is stopping you from being a recycler, even in the garden.

Why throw them out if you can plant them up?

If you can't decide between edible and ornamental, nasturtiums are both.

Eclectic innovations are not for the faint of heart. With small spaces come innovative ideas, and though they're not always suited to everyone's tastes, they do the job, making do with the space you have, the materials most accessible, practicality and functionality. The sky is the limit when it comes to the most eclectic small space gardening ideas. It sounds cliché, but all one really requires is a good imagination and the ability to let go of any ideas of perfection when it comes to aesthetics. Maybe you've seen the plant in an old boot in gardening magazines as kitsch, but why not? Plant up an old pair of rubber boots for fun. It may not be to everyone's taste, but as long as the plant is growing happily and puts a smile on your face, I say go forth and garden unconventionally!

Focus and Style

Not unlike any other garden setting, it's important to determine what your focus and style for your small garden space will be. You're inspired and the ideas are flowing, but with limited space, you have to focus your ideas. Do you want vegetables or fruit to harvest throughout the growing season? Do you want to accentuate or accessorize the space in question? Make it pretty, so to speak? How about a combination of the two—edible and pretty? And once you've decided on your focus, you need to think about your style. Are your tastes more formal or informal? Are you a traditionalist or a modernist? Do you prefer really clean lines or a mish-mash of everything? Are you eclectic in your style or a minimalist?

People often assume there isn't enough room or light to grow much of anything in small residential urban spaces. However, with the diversity of plants available, there are few spaces that wouldn't support some kind of plant. Certainly your choices may be limited as a result of certain factors, but you'll never be completely without choice.

Your location may only have enough room for one pot, but you can choose an elegant, contemporary or kitschy container, something with immense appeal and built-in practicality. Maybe there is only room in your outdoor space to grow a single specimen, or a small selection of plants, and you would prefer to eat some or all of what you've grown, but the light levels are low as the space is exposed to only two or three hours of direct southern sunlight. It may sound impossible, but there are plants for this scenario as well, such as leafy greens in successive crops, or a container filled with a variety of herbs. It may not be an ideal space, but it is a workable space.

It's also important to consider accessibility. If the space is only accessible from a standard-sized door that leads to a small balcony, avoid choosing something incredibly large, heavy or prickly. Not only will it prove difficult to transport a plant with any of these characteristics, but it could become hazardous as well.

Often your decorating style for your inside space will transfer to your garden, whether it's a conscious choice or not. If you remain unsure about the style you're going for, look for inspiration in your life such as favourite places you've travelled, how you dress, friends and family's gardens you admire. And of course, I wouldn't be a self-respecting garden writer if I didn't recommend the thousands of books, magazines and websites available. Also think about memories

Look for inspiration in your life when making style choices.

from your gardening past. Sometimes elements of a childhood garden are the direction you may want to go, and even if it was an expansive veggie garden in your family's yard, there's no reason you can't flavour your current garden space with elements from your memories.

The Importance of Focus

The following is a hypothetical example illustrating the importance of focus when shopping for plants. Joe goes to the garden centre looking for plants for his tiny balcony. He's done all of his homework and knows the amount of light and exposure his balcony gets, and he's taken into consideration details such as the location of the balcony doors, the two-chair bistro set in the corner and the better view of the park across the street on the east side. Joe wants to grow vegetables on his balcony, and all of the boxes on his criteria list have been ticked, so it looks good. He has a few vegetables in mind, and he has the dimensions in which he could plant into two large containers on the balcony floor, one vertical container such as an upside-down tomato planter, and another hanging basket above the bistro set.

But Joe has to go through the annuals and perennials sections of the garden centre to get to the fruit and vegetable section, and while he passes through he fixes his gaze on a very stately, tall, modern planter already planted up with large tropical and annual plants, including a centrepiece vine in the middle staked up with an ornate obelisk. The plants growing in this container are stunning, but they're all going to grow much, much larger—as tall or taller than the central obelisk, and wider than the container that is already borderline too large for his balcony.

Stay focused when you go to the garden centre.

Now we'll all be in this position at least once, and some of us have even acted upon an ill-advised impulse…ahem, not me of course…and regretted it. Joe can't take his eyes off of this planter. Even after measuring it he's certain it will fit on and is well-suited to his balcony.

He'll just forgo the vegetable container ideas, he decides. This is where the denial comes in; even after quickly checking the mature sizes the plants in the container can grow to, and how heavy the container will be to transport up six flights, Joe decides to go ahead.

This large container adds drama to a front yard but would not be appropriate for an apartment balcony.

I'm sure you can figure out the rest of this hypothetical scenario. The container was a nightmare to get up into the apartment, much less onto the balcony. It was too large for the space, and the plants in it only got larger as the season went on. And it threw off the balance and overall appeal of the space because it dwarfed the comfy eating area and didn't provide him with any of the delicious treats he'd so looked forward to. As a final insult, now he was left with a huge container that he really couldn't use again.

It is so incredibly easy to get distracted, even overwhelmed when walking into a garden centre. My advice is to try your best to stay focused while enjoying all it has to offer, and to come prepared with a pretty good, if not exact, theme or idea in mind. If you aren't able to sort out the choices on your own, ask for help. Often garden centre staff is very well trained and experienced, and they'll help you to narrow down the selection if you haven't already done so. This focus will be worth the effort, even though I know it can be hard surrounded by such beauty and inspiration.

Knowing your garden space will help you get the most out of it.

Evaluating Your Garden Space

A little knowledge about your garden space will be critical to the success of the plants you choose. You want to ensure that you're choosing plants appropriate for the space based on light, exposure, space and so on, or are well-equipped to answer questions when asked by garden centre or nursery staff about the space in question so that they can recommend appropriate plants. Either way, it's a learning experience, and sometimes a bit of an experiment, because even with the keenest observations we don't always get it just right, particularly in an urban space where buildings are close together and create unique microclimates, as one example.

Regardless of the space and what it has to offer, you can have a prolific and thriving garden. The only thing you absolutely have to have tucked in your tool belt is a lofty set of realistic expectations. Unrealistic expectations have driven more than a few disappointed gardeners into other pastimes and hobbies. It is important to do your homework long before getting started, and here is how the evaluation comes into play.

If you only have a location that gets less than two hours of sunlight, you're best not to select sun-loving plants that rely upon that energy to thrive and produce fruit and vegetables. You'll only end up with stretched, faded plants and no fruit or vegetables. Or how about if you have a south-facing balcony, six stories up and surrounded by other high-rises, one block from the beach. It's likely going to be intensely hot and exposed to everything Mother Nature has to throw at it, including salty wind blowing through the wind tunnel that forms between the surrounding walls of high-rises. Only the toughest, sun- and heat-loving plants, adept to withstand high winds and full exposure, are warranted for this location. These are just two of the infinite combinations that have to be evaluated because without the necessary information on which to base plant selections, you'll end

up disappointed and your plants will wish they'd never left the garden centre.

So where do you start? Let's break it down into the criteria that need to be determined when observing the location you've chosen to grow plants. Each location will be different from the next because few of the elements affecting plants will be exactly the same in any two locations.

Climate and Microclimate

First, know your climate. Overall, Canada is a fantastic country in which to garden, though the cold winter weather and potentially short growing season in many regions do present some challenges. A wealth of diverse growing conditions is found here—almost every imaginable gardening situation short of tropical is experienced somewhere in the country. The adjacent oceans significantly modify the climate on both the East Coast and the West Coast, resulting

Cold Canadian winters do present gardening challenges, but nothing that can't be overcome.

in more moderate winter temperatures and cooler summers, as well as fog, salty air and, often, thin, rocky, acidic soils.

Warm summers and cold winters dominate in most of eastern and central Canada, and the climate is modified by each region's proximity to water. The floodplains that border the St. Lawrence River are fertile and deep. Gardeners on the Canadian Shield around Hudson Bay generally have acidic and fertile but rocky soils, and those living around Georgian Bay and the Great Lakes may have sandy or rocky soils. Southern Ontario has mostly alkaline, less rocky soil and milder winters, thanks to the moderating effect of the Great Lakes.

The cold winters of the Prairies are hard on tender perennial plants, but the sun-filled days of summer encourage plant growth. The soils can be clay, sand or loam, and they tend to be alkaline. The Rocky Mountains have short, often dry summers and cold winters. The valleys between the mountains are often more temperate, and there is no shortage of gardeners to take advantage of the best their region has to offer. The North, though sparsely populated, has its share of determined gardeners as well. The varied geography shares many traits with adjacent Rockies and Prairies, but typically the North has thin, acidic soils, low levels of precipitation, scattered permafrost, very cold winters and a short growing season.

Day length varies from one region to another depending on the distance from the equator and the season. This variance enables plants to determine when to enter into a flowering cycle. So, if a plant requiring short or long day lengths to flower is growing in a location near the equator, it will remain in a vegetative state, without flowers. It is important to consider a plant's location prior to planting it. Plants have their own way of "knowing" or sensing subtle changes in temperature and light, which is partly why I am so fascinated with plants and nature in general. This sense enables plants to flower and fruit at the right time and tells them when to go into dormancy and when to come alive again after a winter sleep. It truly is amazing how they are able to differentiate one season from another. However, a plant in the wrong location can get confused, which is one of many reasons that a plant will be successful in one location but not in another. Apple trees, for example, grow best in regions with cool climates because they have evolved over time to require a sequence of warm days with cooler temperatures at night to reawaken after a winter dormancy, signalling a flowering cycle. In regions without cool nights, apple trees aren't able to flower properly, which negatively affects fruit production.

Despite these regional characteristics and limitations, conditions can deviate greatly from garden to garden within a region. In addition to broad factors such as climate, season length and day length, the details of soil conditions, garden microclimates, light and heat influence your garden regardless of where you are in Canada. These can vary not only from garden to garden but also within a single garden.

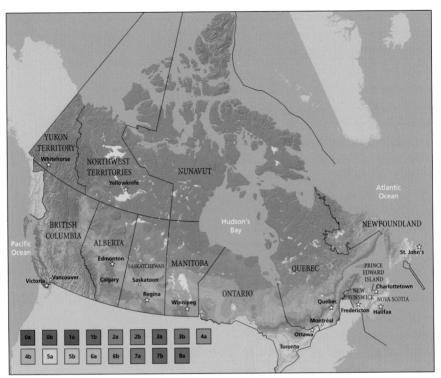

Hardiness zones (above); average annual frost free days (below)

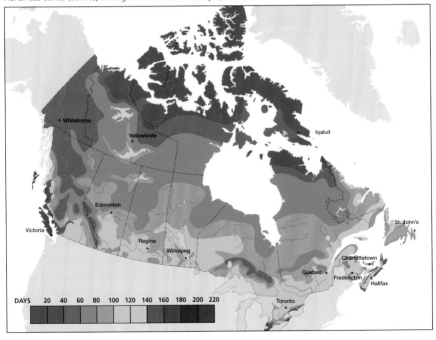

The three most important pieces of climate information for Canadian gardeners are the hardiness zone, the last frost date of spring and the first frost date of fall. These are not hard and fast rules but are excellent guidelines that will help you pick plants and plan your garden. Hardiness zones (see map, top left) are relevant mostly for perennials, trees and shrubs. Plants are rated based on the lowest hardiness zone they will grow in. The average number of frost-free days (see map, bottom left) is a good estimate of season length. If you can only depend on four frost-free months, you may want to choose plants that will survive a light frost or that will mature during your anticipated growing season.

This information provides a good starting point but should not completely rule your planting decisions. Microclimates can affect temperatures, causing plants to react differently in one location compared to another. Choose plants that suit the microclimates in your garden.

Light

There are four basic levels of light in a garden: full sun, partial sun (partial shade), light shade and full shade. Buildings, trees, fences, walls and the position of the sun at different times of the day and year affect available light. Full sun locations, such as along south-facing walls, receive more than six hours of direct sunlight during the day. Locations classified as partial shade/sun, such as east- or west-facing walls, receive direct sunlight for part of the day (four to six hours) and shade for the rest. Light shade locations receive shade for most or all of the day, though some sunlight does filter through to ground level. An example of a light shade location might be the ground under a small-leaved tree. Full shade locations, which can include the north side of a house, receive no direct sunlight.

It may take a few days, but check in on the space you'll be gardening in throughout the day, from sunrise to

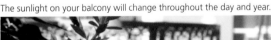

The sunlight on your balcony will change throughout the day and year.

nightfall. It's important to remember that the amount of light your space receives will change over the season, and every space will have its own subtle differences. Record which direction the space faces: north, south, east or west, or a combination of two. Record what is in the immediate vicinity, especially things that may obscure or block light from the area, such as surrounding buildings, balconies, fences, trees, etc. Take note of how those features change the light in the area throughout the day. Just because a location is south facing doesn't mean it will receive full sun from sunrise to sundown. There may be a tree on the east side that is preventing the sun from hitting the area until the afternoon, and what is being permitted to trickle through is dappled. The balcony above may be blocking much of the afternoon sun, making it more shaded than sunny. A space such as this may only really have intense sunlight from 2 PM onward but dappled to shaded sunlight for the rest of the day. Or perhaps it receives light shade from sunrise to 9 AM, then changes to intense or full sun from 9:30 AM to noon, only to be shaded from then until 4 or 5 PM, with a partly sunny late afternoon until dusk. Recording from hour to hour how the light changes will provide you with a very clear picture of how sunny or shaded the area really is.

Exposure

The space you've chosen to grow plants in may be exposed to wind, heat, cold and rain, and some plants are better adapted than others to withstand the potential damage of these forces. Buildings, walls, fences, hills, hedges and trees influence and often reduce exposure.

Wind and heat are the most likely elements to cause damage. The sun can be very intense, and heat can rise quickly on a sunny afternoon. Choose plants that tolerate or even thrive in hot weather for the hot spaces.

Overwatering or too much rain can be damaging. Early in the season, seeds or seedlings can be washed away or drowned in heavy rain; mulch around the seeded area will help prevent this problem. Established plants can also be

Hanging baskets are often quite exposed to the elements.

damaged by heavy rain. Most plants will recover, but some are slow to do so. Waterlogged soil can encourage root rot on plants that prefer well-drained soil. Place sensitive plants in protected areas, or choose plants that are quick to recover from rain damage.

You'll have to observe your area so that you have a clear idea of how it is exposed to wind and other elements. If you compare a balcony that sticks out from the outer wall of the building to one that is nicely tucked into a pocket, the likelihood is that the first balcony would be much more exposed to the wind, as would the plants growing on it. Some plants are keen to be in such an exposed site; others will not do well. This type of observation applies to exposure of other elements as well. If you're on the East Coast, for example, where storms have an intensity unlike those farther inland, then the rain alone may do damage to delicate plants in fully exposed areas; if you're on the Prairies, hailstorms in late summer can cause damage to exposed plants. If the area you're considering is a wind tunnel, make sure to choose plants that can tolerate the conditions without being shredded apart or knocked over.

Pollution

Pollution is present to varying degrees in every urban and rural setting, but likely more so in the city. In order to have the healthiest plants, particularly those that are producing food for harvest, you want to ensure that they have potting mixes or soils free of toxins. You cannot control the air quality, but you can lessen the toxicity of your plants' environment.

If planting directly into the ground, try to determine what was in the location prior to your home. Was it simply virgin land, or was there some type of commercial development in place, such as a service station or shopping centre? Or was the previous tenant or owner a motorcycle mechanic who overhauled his engines directly on the soil? Commercial developments can render the soil unusable for generations, even when reclaimed. And far too often people just don't realize what kind of damage they

Grow your edibles in containers if your garden soil is contaminated.

may be causing to the soil. Chemical contaminants don't simply leave with the commercial business or previous resident.

If you're unable to determine the life of the soil previous to you moving in, and you are going to be planting directly into the ground, then I highly recommend a soil test. Inexpensive test kits are available at garden centres, or you can go for a more in-depth test from a testing facility. These tests are usually available in larger municipalities, either as an extension of a university with an agriculture or horticulture department or from an independent, privately owned company. The cost is minimal and the results are priceless because often they are accompanied by instructions on how to amend the soil to make it balanced and ready for planting.

Lastly, be aware of possible pathways of pollution, such as driveways and streetside near exhaust pipes, or in raised beds made with railway ties or treated wood. Not all treated wood is toxic, however, so ask your local supplier about the best type of wood to use if you're considering building raised beds.

Space

One very important step in evaluating your garden space is to measure the space you've chosen for your garden. Measure for length, width, height and even depth. This combination will provide you with a guideline, or a boundary never to cross. Bring these measurements with you when you go to the garden centre.

Height can be a limiting factor in urban spaces, particularly if you're planning on gardening on your balcony. The area will be surrounded by a railing, but also often by the ceiling of a balcony above your own. Measure both the height of the railing and the height from floor to ceiling, if a ceiling exists. If the area in question is out in the open, free of anything surrounding it, such as on a terrace or patio

Measure your garden space before you head to the garden centre.

in a tiny townhouse or condo backyard, then a measure of height is not necessary.

If you're considering planting things vertically, then take measurements for that as well, such as the height of the wall you're planning to use. With hanging baskets, it doesn't hurt to measure the width of the space from the centre outward (the radius). Hanging baskets planted by garden centre staff are usually meant to impress, and often that is done not only with colour but also with density and size. Just because it's a certain width when you purchase it in May doesn't mean it's going to stay that size. It may triple in size over the growing season, depending on what type of plants are in the basket, and how many.

Make sure to take foot traffic and seating areas, if any, into account. It's all well and good to have enough space for your plants, but it's also important to have enough space for you. You will have to get in and out of the space on a daily basis, and you may even want to spend time in that

space. It could prove to be quite aggravating to want to eat breakfast each morning on your balcony, at that adorable little bistro set you so carefully chose, only to find that the containers and plants have left you with no room to lift fork to mouth.

It is far better to have too many measurements than not enough. It never fails to amaze me every time someone asks me what would be best for their garden, but they have no idea how large the space is. I can guarantee that nine out of ten guesses are wrong. Sometimes it is also helpful to take a measurement of the balcony doors. It may save a huge headache in the end.

Weight

Weight is very important when evaluating the criteria for a garden, especially when growing plants on a balcony, deck, rooftop or raised patio. The consolidated weight of soil or planting mixes, water, containers and the plants themselves

Weight may be a limiting factor for a balcony garden.

can result in a quite a heavy load. Granted most balconies and so on are built to hold hefty sums of weight, but we're never really told exactly how much, or for how long. Maybe the building is old or has been poorly maintained, or the balcony is tiny and not capable of supporting more than two people and a few containers.

It's best to check with the landlord, builder or management company if you're unsure about the weight limit for your balcony. There are ways to reduce the weight of your garden as well. For example, if you're using containers, stay away from heavy materials such as stone, concrete, pottery and even wood and go for resin, plastic or fibreglass. They're readily available, have come down exponentially in price and are as light as a feather. They also come in just about every colour and style you could possibly imagine and can

be incredibly convincing when made to look like something else, whether it be stone or pottery. Soil-less potting mixes are not only lightweight but also better for the plants when in containers. Placing some of your containers on railings or mounting them on walls is a good way to distribute the weight, taking some of it off of the floor of the balcony and balancing it over the whole space.

Containers vs. Raised Beds

Now there is only one last thing to consider: in what are you going to grow the plants? Are containers your only option? Do you have a little plot of soil in the ground to work with? Do you have enough space to accomodate a raised bed? Or do you only have wall space to work with?

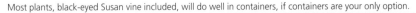

Most plants, black-eyed Susan vine included, will do well in containers, if containers are your only option.

When you have the choice between growing plants in containers and growing directly in the ground or in raised beds, which option will make best use of the space you have? Or maybe you don't have any choice at all because your balcony, deck, patio or rooftop simply won't accommodate anything other than containers.

This is where you put into play all of the elements you've gathered together to make the urban garden happen. You've chosen what type of style you want, and you've evaluated the area, so now you have to determine how it will be executed: in-ground/raised beds or containers, or a combination of the two. There are pros and cons for any type of garden.

The Pros and Cons of Containers

Growing plants in containers is a wonderful way to optimize your space. Containers mean you can create a garden in the smallest of spaces—on balconies, decks, patios, teeny-tiny backyards and even spaces you didn't even think possible, such as walls, front steps, window ledges, railings or a ceiling overhang. Container gardening makes almost any space into a space for growing.

Certainly one of the biggest advantages to container gardening is the flexibility it allows. Containers allow you to move things around as you see fit, and to switch up the plants in them on a whim. When you have nothing but a fixed space, with flower or vegetable beds already set out, you're basically forced to comply with what is already in place. Sure you could fill beds in, expand them or move them around, but it takes quite a lot of sweat equity and time to do so. With container gardening, versatility is the key. There is no reason why you have to do the same thing twice in containers. You can create a whole new look every year simply by rearranging the containers and changing the plantings.

Ease of movement is especially ideal when growing vegetables. Spinach, for example, likes a lot of sun in the earlier parts of spring, but in the hot summer sun it tends to bolt. If you plant your spinach in a container, you could keep it in your sunniest spot for spring and then move the pot into a partly shaded location for summer, thus keeping the plants from bolting and extending your spinach season. As an added bonus,

With the right containers and the right plants, you can grow a garden anywhere.

Peppers will do better in containers than in the ground.

poor plot design, it doesn't take long for soil to become compacted and compromised, causing your plants to struggle. In containers, soil compaction is rarely an issue. Your plants' roots are able to move freely to absorb moisture and nutrients, ensuring healthy, vibrant growth.

If you hate weeding and are tired of the damage pests cause in more traditional garden settings, almost all of these problems are eliminated with container gardening. Weeding will become a rare experience. Often the only weeds that come up are from the odd seed blown in that germinates along with your intentional plantings. And many of the pests that cause damage in in-ground plots simply aren't present in containers. Cutworms, for example, are often present in the soil and come back from one year to the next. In containers, you use brand new potting mix every year that is not contaminated with pests or disease. Any pests that do attack container gardens are much easier to control because they're usually in smaller numbers and at easier reach than garden bed infestations.

There is no other gardening environment where you have more control. One major aspect of this control is the soil or potting mix itself. You choose what kind to put into the container, and often it's sterile, light and airy. You can even cater to certain plant groupings with different types of mixes.

Again, this control over potting mix is particularly important for vegetables. When you're growing vegetables in the ground, it is critical to rotate your crops from year to year, but maybe your garden

moving the spinach out of the full sun real estate will make room for heat-loving vegetables, such as peppers. And if your peppers are not quite ripe when frost is expected, you can move the container to a sheltered location to extend their growing season into fall.

It's quite common for soil compaction to occur with in-ground plots. Without being careful where you step, and with plot simply isn't big enough. Certain plants may suffer from being in basically the same location year after year. One crop tends to pull a particular set of nutrients from the soil, depending upon its particular needs, or it leaves certain fungi, bacteria and the like behind, lying in wait for the next crop. However, you can grow vegetables in the same pot year after year because you're starting with new potting mix at the beginning of the season.

Obviously there are many benefits to gardening in containers, but there can be some disadvantages too—nothing that can't be overcome, though.

Nutrient depletion in containers can be cause for concern. Because of the small amount of medium or potting mix surrounding the roots of the plants, and because of the frequency of watering containers, nutrients simply get drawn up by the plants or washed out of the pot over time. It is important to integrate organic material into the mix when you're initially planting and to fertilize with an organic, natural fertilizer throughout the growing season. I'll go into this in more detail later on (see Feeding, page 95).

Watering containers can also be challenging in some cases owing to their size and to the potting mix, which is often very light, fluffy and prone to drying out much faster than garden soil. The amount of times you have to water can vary from one week to the next depending on how much the plants have grown, what the temperatures have been like, how much wind exposure they're getting and the type of container in which the plants are growing. There are ways to improve water retention, but the bottom line is that you will likely have to water frequently throughout the growing season.

Nutrient depletion can be a problem in small containers.

Size limitations can be another disadvantage of container gardening. Always keep in mind that the containers you choose for your urban garden have to be easy enough to move when necessary, not too heavy for certain areas including balconies, raised decks and patios, but also large enough to house whatever you're planting. Flowering annuals and vegetable plants have a relatively short lifespan, and they can be a little crowded and still do well. Long-term plants, however, need adequate space, and finding the balance between too much and not enough is key. A small tree in a pot, for example, will need space to grow. It may be fine in its original pot at first, but year after year its rootball will expand, and it will eventually need to be repotted into a larger container. Perhaps that container weighs 50 pounds

This shrub will eventually need a bigger container.

empty—just imagine what it will weigh when it's full of soil and the plant, not to mention the moisture added weekly, if not daily. And then two years later it will need an even bigger pot. Is the bigger pot (and bigger plant) simply going to be too big for the space overall? Or maybe a safety issue for those below? These factors are important to consider when you're thinking of going big.

Lastly, plants in any gardening situation need to be well taken care of, but keeping plants in container gardens happy can be challenging. It doesn't take much for container plants to become stressed. Either they are allowed to dry out to the extreme too often, or they are forced to contend with inadequate drainage and left to sit in pools of water for too long, working toward rot, or they must struggle to survive with depleted nutrient sources, no fertilizer in sight. All of these things can slowly break a plant down, just as we can get run down by not getting enough sleep, not eating our vegetables and dealing with too much stress. Just like us, plants become vulnerable, and there's nothing more attractive to pests and disease than a stressed and weak plant. It is important to keep plants healthy, and this may take some effort on your part. Trust me, it's worth it.

You can grow just about anything in a container, in just about any place, but the positives and negatives listed above show just how important it is to choose the right plant for the right conditions. Containers are made of just about every material you can think of these days, and they all react differently to the various elements thrown at them. Some retain heat more than others; some seem to lose water as fast as you can give it to them, while others actually help to maintain the moisture in the mix for longer periods. The trick is to discover which containers work for which plants, and doing so may take some trial and error. Granted sometimes it may not work out, but experimentation is part of the process. Every location is unique to the next, and the only way you'll be able to determine what is best for that space, and for you, is to try; you may fail, but that is part of the learning process, and it can be a lot of fun.

Container Materials

Containers are constructed from a number of different materials including clay, metal, wood, stone and plastic, fibreglass and other synthetics. Be aware that some container materials are more suitable for our Canadian climate than others.

Some materials are more appropriate for certain containers. Window boxes are usually made out of wood or plastic. It is possible to use stone or metal, but weight would be a critical determining factor. Wooden window boxes can also be custom built to blend in with the building's architecture. Hanging baskets are most often constructed of wood or wire, with weight again being a determining factor. There are a number of attractive stands available that provide sturdy support for hanging baskets.

Clay

Clay pots come in two basic forms— glazed and unglazed—in a plethora of shapes and sizes. Clay pots can be heavy, even when they are empty. They can be

Just about anything can be used as a container.

damaged by cold weather and require special care in most parts of Canada, in areas that freeze up rather solidly in winter as well as in areas that experience numerous freeze/thaw cycles. The irresistible draw of clay pots is that they age beautifully over time like no other container material will. Within a few seasons, a combination of salts and organic growth will build on the walls of the pot, resulting in a lovely patina.

Unglazed clay pots are often referred to as *terracotta,* which simply means "baked earth," referring to the kiln-firing process used in making the pots. Terracotta containers are somewhat porous, which allows the plant roots to breathe easily but also allows for the quick evaporation of moisture, so they require frequent monitoring and watering. Given their porosity, terracotta pots should be soaked before planting. If the container is not soaked first, the clay will draw the moisture out of the soil and away from your new plants. Terracotta holds heat into the night longer than wood, metal or synthetics. Be aware that terracotta containers come in different qualities, and you often get what you pay for. Terracotta pots from Italy and other Mediterranean countries are usually very good quality.

Glazed clay containers offer another way to incorporate colour into the overall design scheme of your garden. Glazed containers are not porous, so they will need a few drainage holes on or near the bottom but will not need to be soaked prior to planting. Glazed pots also benefit from a plastic lining, which helps to prevent cracking if moisture seeps in.

Wood

Wooden containers are very adaptable and can be custom built to fit into their surroundings. Wood offers more insulating value than clay, metal and stone, but it is susceptible to rot, so containers are often lined with plastic or coated with a non-toxic wood preservative. Some woods, such as cedar (*Arborvitae* spp.), are relatively rot resistant. Do not use wood that has been treated with creosote or other toxic substances that can emit compounds that can harm your plants.

Wood is very amiable to our climate and can be used across the country. Make sure the containers are of sturdy construction. If you have wooden barrels, make sure the hoops and handles are firmly attached. To ensure the longevity of your wooden containers, protect them with wood stain, particularly at the joints and seams, or wood oils, both of which enhance the natural grain and prevent it

Terracotta

Wood

from cracking. Linseed oil is the best oil to use to protect wood that is prone to drying out.

Stone

Stone includes terrazzo, concrete, reconstructed or refurbished stone and natural stone. Stone containers are available in a vast array of shapes, sizes, styles and colours. They tend to be heavy and difficult to move. It is best to plant stone containers after they are set in their relatively permanent location, unless they've been placed atop a strong platform or cart with wheels. Stone is often used to accent gardens, and aggregate planters allow stone to be seen on the container surface. Carved stone pots can be very expensive but will add a level of elegance to any formal container garden. A large rock with a trough makes a wonderful place for tiny alpine plants but may need drainage holes drilled through the stone. Concrete containers, as well as reconstructed and refurbished stone containers, can be cast in many forms. Stone containers are suitable for all areas of Canada.

If you're going for an elegantly aged look for your garden, you can accelerate the aging process on the exterior of your stone containers by simply rubbing a fistful of fresh grass across the surface of the pot. The stain will quickly fade to brown. Brushing a thin layer of yogurt onto a pot's surface will encourage algae and lichen to grow, but a shady and moist location is necessary for the best result.

Stone (above and below)

Metal

Metal containers can be made from tin, copper, bronze, iron, steel or lead, and they range from simple buckets to fancy, ornate planters and urns. Be aware that metal pots absorb heat like dark-coloured containers do. Most metal pots should be lined with plastic to protect them from contact with the soil, which will prolong the life of the container. Or, rather than using a lining, plants in plastic containers can be inserted into decorative metal containers. Make sure your metal containers have adequate drainage holes. To protect the drainage holes from rust, apply a coat of anti-rust paint.

To maintain the bright, reflective surfaces of your metal pots, use a soft cloth and window-cleaning spray. Do not use abrasive pads or cleaners. Be careful not to splash water or potting mix onto polished metal; the splashes may leave white calcium deposits, but they can be removed with a soft cloth.

Wire is used to make cage-like frames such as hanging baskets, planters

Metal

and ornate plant stands that can double as planters. These frames are lined with sphagnum moss or some other suitable material before being planted.

Synthetics

The most commonly used synthetic materials for containers are plastic and fibreglass. These containers come in a vast range of shapes and sizes, from whimsical plastic duck and teddy bear planters to the newer fibreglass containers that resemble terracotta pots. Synthetic containers are not permeable, so they will need drainage holes. They are lightweight and easy to move with minimal concern for breakage, and most of them are good quality and inexpensive. Some lower-quality plastic containers can deteriorate in the sunlight.

Synthetic containers are a good choice for the apartment or condo dweller. They are lightweight and well suited for use on a balcony, and they can be easily moved in and out of storage seasonally.

Plastic

Self-watering Containers

This type of container is available just about everywhere in Canada, in garden centres and box stores. Self-watering containers come in a wide range of materials, sizes and colours but are somewhat restrictive in style and sometimes lack originality; however, they're not designed for looks. They're designed to conserve water, and they do so in a very simple way. A reservoir underneath the rootball is filled with water. The water is then wicked up through a wicking basket into the potting mix as the plant(s) growing in the container require it. Depending on a variety of factors, including the size of plant(s) growing in the container, the weather, the type of potting mix, etc., the water is usually drawn up quite slowly, requiring less trips to the container with a watering can and less water overall. It's an incredibly useful system. The containers can come at a cost, but I think they're well worth the extra money because of the water and labour saved over time.

This method of water conservation is not much different in principle from using a soaker hose in an in-ground or raised bed. When you water from the top of a container, much of the water runs right though the potting mix and drains away through the bottom of the container. A self-watering container, like a soaker hose, keeps the water at the roots of the plant.

There are other types of self-watering set-ups, and many of those methods are described online. Most pertain to a homemade, single pot method, but there are some that will water several pots at once.

Self-watering systems are definitely worth exploring. With a little creativity and ingenuity, I'm sure anyone could build a system capable of reducing the quantity of water used throughout the growing season, which is not only easier on the pocket book but also easier on the back, and on the environment.

Making Your Own Self-watering Container

If you're feeling a little adventurous, you can make your own self-watering container. Doing so is relatively easy; it requires only a few, inexpensive materials, and the results are well worth the effort. If you can let go of aesthetics a little, a homemade self-watering system is a great solution for excessive water usage, and here's how you do it.

The Materials

- 2 five-gallon, food-safe buckets
- 1 small (500 mL) plastic container
- PVC pipe, 1" (2.5 cm) diameter and slightly longer than the height of the buckets when they are stacked one inside the other
- wooden dowelling, ½" (1.25 cm) diameter and same length as pipe (diameter can be less, but not more)
- drill and drill bits
- jigsaw
- zip ties

The Assembly

- Turn one bucket upside down. Drill several ¼" holes in the bottom of the bucket for drainage.

- Position the plastic container over the centre of the bottom of the bucket. Trace around the container, and then draw another circle about ⅛" inside the first circle.

- Using a standard drill bit, make a starter hole just inside the inner line, large enough to accomodate the blade of the jigsaw. Use the jigsaw to carefully cut around the inner line, leaving outer line intact. The plastic container should fit inside the hole, with its rim resting on the edge and keeping it from falling through.

- Position the PVC pipe over the bottom of the bucket, off to the side of the centre hole, and trace around it. Use the drill and jigsaw to carefully cut around that line.

- Drill several ¼" holes in the sides of the plastic container—only the sides, not the bottom. Then drill three or four more holes close to the rim of the container, with corresponding holes in the bucket. Secure the container to the bucket with zip ties. The container is now your wicking basket.

- Insert the altered bucket into the unaltered bucket, so that they are nested together.

- Measure the height of the stacked buckets. Cut the PVC pipe and dowelling to be at least 1" longer than the measured height. Cut one end of the pipe at an angle to allow water to move freely in and out of the pipe.

- Insert the pipe into the hole in the bucket, angled end down, to function as a watering tube through which you'll fill the water reservoir—the space left between the two buckets.

- Insert the dowelling into the pipe. The dowel will act as a water level indicator. If it is bobbing slightly higher than the pipe, you know there is water in the reservoir, but if it is flush with the pipe, you know the reservoir is empty.
- Drill a hole in the outer bucket, approximately ¼" below where the bottom of the inner bucket rests. This hole will allow for drainage of excess water from the reservoir, just in case the whole assembly was to get saturated during a rainstorm, or just gets too much water from the hose.
- Fill the reservoir up by adding water to the pipe until the dowel is bobbing and water starts to spill out the reservoir's drainage hole.
- Fill roughly half of the inner bucket with potting mix, and plant it up.

With this self-watering container system, you'll likely find that you only have to water twice weekly rather than every day, depending on the weather and what is growing in the container, and at what stage it is growing. I'll go more into the benefits and importance of water conservation later on (see page 108), but for now, just keep in mind that anything that saves water is a good thing.

The Pros and Cons of Raised Beds

If you have a townhouse or rowhouse, then you'll likely have a bit of a green space, including a tiny in-ground plot in which to plant. I suggest raised beds rather than simply growing directly in the ground. Aptly named, raised beds are growing beds raised above ground level. The soil is contained by walls, and those walls can be made of wood, concrete, metal, stone or plastic. Often raised beds are made with wood, particularly when constructed by the resident or home owner. The walls aren't necessary to complete a raised bed, but it just makes sense to contain the soil to prevent erosion, and they nicely define the space.

When the opportunity for growing in the ground is present, why build a raised bed right on top, you might ask. There are a variety of benefits to raised beds. One is the ability to remedy soil compaction and/or contaminated soil. It's not uncommon for garden plots to become very compacted, particularly in certain regions where soils are primarily made up of clay. Building a raised bed on top of this type of location allows for one to

plant in lighter, fluffier mixes that resist compaction, allow for proper drainage and are sterile, free of pollution and contaminants. Raised beds also allow people to grow where no soil was present to begin with, such as atop a hard surface including driveways, patios and so on.

Planting in a raised bed is really like direct planting, but by raising the ground up, you extend the season by a few sometimes crucial days because the soil warms faster in spring. The higher level also makes maintenance easier. You have better control over the mix within the walls of the bed and can easily amend the mix

Raised beds offer many benefits to pants.

annually without the need for rototilling, double-digging or any other labour-intensive digging methods. The need for weeding is greatly reduced because you don't have to contend with all the weed seeds present in regular garden soil. And although raised beds may have to be watered more frequently because of being raised above the ground, that's a small con compared to all the pros.

Raised beds can experience pest and disease problems, but they are remarkably reduced compared to those in a traditional in-ground plot. Diseases are less likely to take hold because the soil mix is replenished from one growing season to the next, and because the bed is raised above the actual soil level, even many of the pest problems in standard plots are alleviated.

Most importantly, raised beds are ideal for gardeners with physical mobility issues who can't bend and squat as easily as they used to, or at all. Depending on the height and width of the bed, the gardener can gently lean into the garden by either sitting or leaning on the edge, rather than having to get down to the ground. Raised beds can save your back, knees and a whole list of aches and pains, and they allow people who might have given up gardening a chance to get their hands dirty once again, and for years to come.

Raised beds can make maintenance easier.

There aren't many cons to raised beds, but if forced to come up with something, I would have to say that compared to containers, raised beds do require some assembly, the amount and difficulty of which depends on the style and whether you're building them from scratch or from a kit. Raised beds are also semi-permanent. If you ever move, the raised bed won't be coming along. If you rent rather than own your property, you might also require permission from management or a strata council or condo board to build a raised bed, and even then bylaws sometimes won't allow for structures of this kind to be built on any common property. Otherwise, if raised beds are allowed, constructed with the right materials and are the right size to meet your needs, then the list attributed to raised beds is overwhelmingly pro.

Building Your Own Raised Bed

It is super easy to build a raised bed. There are kits on the market that only require some easy assembly and are often inexpensive, providing the supplies necessary to put it all together in no time flat. You can also draw up your own plan and gather the necessary supplies yourself. Doing so is equally inexpensive and has the advantage of being sure to

Building a stone raised bed can be expensive, but the result is lovely.

fit the space you have because you are custom building it for that space. The beauty of raised beds is that you can make them to your own specifications.

One thing I did was to build three fantastic raised beds in my parents' backyard in the place where the traditional vegetable garden plot was. It was becoming much too difficult for any of us to find the time or energy to maintain such a large space. All the watering, weeding and cultivating was taking a toll. I built the raised beds directly on top of the garden. They are just the right size for someone to sit or lean on the side walls and be able to gently lean into the middle to seed, water, weed or harvest. These beds make it possible for my parents to garden a little, without straining their backs and knees. I lined the paths in between the beds with layer after layer of newspaper and a thick layer of bark mulch. I replenish it yearly to keep it thick to prevent weeds and grass from coming up, and it makes for a nice surface to walk on.

Raised beds should be built to allow the gardener to reach into the centre without much effort, so widths of 90 cm–1.2 m are average. Any wider and one would be reaching and stretching to get to the middle, or might need to step into the bed, which would defeat the purpose. The length of the bed doesn't matter really, as long as the walls are supported to prevent them from bowing out from the pressure of the soil within the bed.

The other size consideration to take into account, aside from width and length, is height. To determine the ideal height, consider what you want to plant,

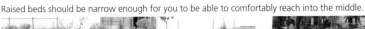

Raised beds should be narrow enough for you to be able to comfortably reach into the middle.

for example vegetables, and how deep a soil they require. Leafy vegetables and herbs need only about 15–30 cm of soil depth to thrive, though deeper is fine, while root vegetables require deeper beds to produce roots worth harvesting. Either the height of the bed needs to be at least 60 cm to accommodate root vegetables, or the soil under the mix in the bed can be cultivated to allow for more depth. I find that building the walls up is better if for no other reason than accessibility. Also, deeper beds allow you to have the option of changing your mind from one season to the next, while shallow beds leave you with fewer choices of what to plant.

Wood is a common material to use for building raised beds, but if you're using wood, be cautious of what type you use—not so much for the species, but for what it's been treated with. If you're unsure, ask the staff at the lumber yard or hardware store if the wood has been treated with anything, and if so, whether that product is safe for use as the walls for a bed containing food-producing plants. Treated wood will have a longer life, which will ultimately prolong the life of the bed, but you don't want to put your family at risk. One option is to treat the wood yourself, using products that are both ecologically friendly and food safe, such as tung oil, linseed oil or an eco-based stain. Another option is to go with untreated cedar; it won't rot and is well-suited to this type of application.

Deep raised beads mean you don't have to limit yourself to shallow-rooted plants.

Mulch the pathways between raised beds.

The bottom of the bed does not have to be lined, but it can be if burrowing animals or other critters are an issue. Certain fabrics and wire mesh can aptly do the job. Do not line the bed with plastic. Plastic lining will only cause problems down the line such as rot, poor drainage, excessive heat and no way for the soil to breathe or for microorganisms to move freely between the mix in the raised bed and the soil underneath. It's usually unnecessary to line the bed.

Support the walls using thick wooden stakes or PVC pipe. Either of these materials can be cut longer than the actual height of the bed so they can be pounded into the ground as anchors, keeping the bed from shifting and the walls from bowing outward.

If you have room for more than one bed, and they're going side by side, make sure to leave enough space for a pathway between them. Ideally, it's nice to have the pathway wide enough to accommodate whatever it is you may use to cart supplies and materials to the beds, such as a wheelbarrow, but certainly there needs to be enough room to walk and move around. A pathway approximately 1 m wide is optimal.

The pathways should be mulched unless you're going to allow grass to grow between, which is perfectly fine. A good layer of mulch will prevent you having to walk in the dirt, or mud if it's been raining. Stones or gravel are one option for a mulching material, but unless the pieces are small, such as road crush, they're not the nicest to walk on. Stone is also heavy and retains heat, and it's expensive because you need a lot, and I mean a lot, to lay a gravel mulch down thick enough to suppress weeds. Any type of rock used as mulch may benefit from a landscape fabric underneath, which may prevent some weeds from coming up, but it won't guarantee a weed-free space. Some persistent weeds are bound to come up, simply because weed seeds blow in from elsewhere. When this happens in any type of rock atop fabric, the seed just begins to grow on top of the fabric in the sediment and so on that is also sitting on top of the fabric. Weeding in any type of gravel is not fun. It's hard on the fingers

Finely cut bark makes an ideal mulch for pathways.

and will grind your fingernails down to the nub.

Bark mulch or any other natural, non-rock type of mulch is great, whether it's pine needles or straw, but it needs to be a material that is comfortable to walk on and that is easily and economically replenished every couple of years because it will break down over time, and you will need to add more here and there to maintain the thickness necessary to suppress most weeds and grass. Often a layer about 5–10 cm thick will do it, but a little more is even better.

I also like to lay something biodegradable down first, such as burlap or jute or a thick layer of newspaper (only with natural dyes though). A layer of any of these materials will act similarly to landscape fabric but will break down naturally. It provides a bit of a base for the mulch so that the mulch is not in direct contact with the soil and won't break down as fast. Once the newspaper or jute has broken down, there is a nice natural, organic base that continues to separate the soil from the mulch, and it makes it much easier to pull the odd weed or bit of grass out from the root. A little tip when weeding in the pathways: wait until it has rained or you've watered. Damp soil is much softer than dry soil, and it will mean you can get the weeds out from the root rather than

breaking them off at the crown, only to have them come up again.

One last alternative that I've seen some people use as mulch is a double layer of heavy landscape fabric along their pathways, without anything on top. The double layer will still allow air and water to move freely through while providing a tough, supportive barrier between your feet and the soil beneath, and if tacked in well, it won't move. The only disadvantage for me is how it looks, but beauty is in the eye of the beholder.

Raised beds can also be raised up above the ground, almost like a table with deep edges. These are ideal for anyone who doesn't want to bend over at all, or can't. Just make sure that there is

There are many ways to build a raised bed, so find a design that works for you.

adequate drainage at the bottom of the table-style boxes, and line the bottom with either landscape fabric or fine nylon screening to prevent the soil from escaping with the water when the beds are draining after a good rain or a soak from the hose. The legs of the bed must be solid enough to support the weight, and the edges of the box should really be no deeper than 30 cm for ease of access.

There are many, many different ways to design and construct a raised bed. The following method is one of the most basic, practical and easy to put together. It's also tough, long-lasting and relatively inexpensive, and the materials are readily available. And of course, if building it from scratch isn't your thing, heaps of different kits are available at garden centres, box stores and online.

Some of the necessary supplies

The Materials

The following supplies are what is required for a 3' x 6' bed, 1' deep.

- Lumber: Lengths and widths of lumber will vary at stores and lumber yards. You will require 2" x 6" lumber in whatever lengths are available, but enough for four pieces 6' long for the sides, and four pieces 3' long for the ends. You will also need enough 4" x 4" lumber for four pieces 18" long for the posts. As mentioned earlier, cedar is preferred but you can always find out what other types of weather resistant, untreated woods are available. Treated wood may also be an option, but again, only if the treatment is food safe.

- Fasteners: There are two options for holding it all together: galvanized spiral nails or galvanized screws. I prefer the screws. Use 3½" long nails or screws. You'll require roughly 30 to 50 of them to complete the project, depending on your accuracy and experience.

- Tools: You'll need a drill if you've chosen to use screws or a hammer if you've chosen to use nails, a heavy mallet, a shovel, a rake, a saw (either a hand saw or a power saw, whichever you're comfortable with) and a level.

The Build

To recap: the bed will be 3' x 6' (90 cm x 1.8 m), but you can make it any length you want. It should not be more than 4' (1.2 m) wide, however, for accessibility reasons. The height can also be higher than 1' (30 cm), but don't go over 3' (90 cm) unless additional bracing is put in place to support the walls. If you require depth beyond the 1' (30 cm) , you can also loosen up the soil in the ground below the bed. It really depends on what you plan on growing. If you don't need extra depth, then move on to the next steps.

- Level out the ground where the bed will be. Starting with a level base will make the final levelling job much, much easier. Use a level. If you're using landscape fabric or some other lining, now is the time to put it down.
- Cut (if not already cut at the store) the 4" x 4" lumber into four pieces 18" long. Sharpen or cut to an angle one end of each length so it can be inserted into the ground a few inches, but the point or angle should be no more than 6" long.
- Cut (if not already cut at the store) the 2" x 6" lumber into the two different lengths: four pieces 6' long, and four pieces 3' long.

- Attach one of the 3' lengths to one of the 4" x 4" posts, so the top edge of the board is flush with the square end of the post. Attach another post to the other end of the board, again so the top edge of the board is flush with the square end of the post. Then attach a second 3' length board under the first board. The boards should be parallel and touching, fastened at both ends to the posts. You've now assembled one short end of the raised bed.
- Repeat with the other two 3' lengths and the other two posts to create the other short end.
- Stand one of the assembled ends on its top edge, so the sharpened ends of the posts are pointing upward.

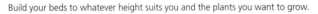

Build your beds to whatever height suits you and the plants you want to grow.

- Attach one of the 6' lengths to one of the assembled short ends so that the long and short boards line up at a perpendicular angle, flush with the square end of the post, to form a corner of the box with the posts on the inside of the walls.

- Fasten the other end of the 6' length to the other assembled short end, again so that the long and short boards line up at a perpendicular angle, flush with the square end of the post, with the posts on the inside of the walls.

- Add another 6' length above the first one. You should now have three walls of the box, with the pointed posts facing the sky.

- Attach the remaining two 6' lengths to the other side to create the fourth wall. Now you should have a complete box.

- Flip the box over so the pointed ends of the posts are making contact with the soil. You may need help to do this safely.

- Pound the posts into the soil a little at a time, alternating to ensure that all the posts are going in evenly; otherwise the box may fracture. Make the box as level as possible, with the bottom edge of the boards flush with the ground, or even slightly underground. If there is a gap between the boards and the ground, the box may lift some when filled, or the soil mix will leak out the gap a little at a time.

- Once the box is in place firmly in the ground, as level as possible and solid, fill your raised bed with the soil mix of your choice. Organic mixes are the best way to go but are not always available in every region. Don't fill the bed up to the very top edge; otherwise the soil will overflow when you plant any type of rootballs or started plants into the bed. You'll also need room to add organic amendments annually, to maintain healthy nutrient levels in the soil. The soil in raised beds can become exhausted over time if not amended and replenished regularly. Now that your raised bed is built and filled, it's only a matter of planting it up and enjoying the fruits of your labour.

Once your bed is built, plant it up and enjoy it.

Planting and Maintaining Your Garden Space

Knowing the basics pertaining to any project is critical to one's success. The basics of plant care are not complicated or labour intensive, but they are important. Much of the following information is specific to gardening in containers, because containers are often what urban gardeners grow stuff in. As much as you are raring to get going, a little time must be spent learning how to keep your plants happy, so read on, urban gardener, read on.

Tools for Urban Gardeners

Gardeners, even those who garden in the smallest of spaces, require their own set of tools. Certainly you won't need as many as someone who gardens in an expansive lot, but the tools you need are not only helpful when growing vegetables on your balcony or flowers in a tight corridor, but they can also be crucial for your gardening successes. As with any task, not having the right tools can make a simple job more difficult, or even dangerous.

Searching for the right tools can be overwhelming in a garden centre or hardware store. It is tough to know where to start, particularly if you are a beginner, and often the sales staff are trying to make a sale, making it difficult to know what is really necessary to bring home. The following is my list of must-have tools for a small urban setting, from in-ground garden spaces and raised beds to container gardening.

All gardeners need a few basic tools and supplies.

Tools for Digging

A **trowel** is a given, whether you're gardening in a raised bed or only containers. It will save your hands, and more specifically your fingers, from the abuse of digging deeply in soil or potting mix. Trowels offer better control when scooping, moving and digging in soil, much more so than any improvised tool. They were designed for just this purpose and are perfect for just about any garden task.

When it comes to tools, you get what you pay for. You can often tell what the quality is like when browsing in person at a store, but be careful if you're buying online unless it's a brand or style you're familiar with. I can't even begin to tell you the trowels I've gone through over the past 20 or more years, simply because I chose cheap over quality. The cheaper ones will almost always bend when digging in firm or hard soils, and once the metal becomes fatigued, it will eventually break. Go with a very hard metal; ideally, the metal should be strong enough not to bend at all. Also, try to find a trowel that is one solid piece, from the scoop right through to the top of the handle, to alleviate some of the pressure where the handle meets the scoop in a trowel made of more than one material.

A comfort grip isn't necessary, but it sure does make it easier on the hands. Make sure that the material covering the metal handle is durable, or you may end up with a naked handle in less than one season. I recommend staying away from any small hand tool with a wooden handle, even if the metal goes through the wooden shaft. Over time, with heat and

Trowel

cold, dry and wet, the wood will shrink and become brittle. As a result, it may crack or become loosened from the metal shaft it surrounds and slip, and then the tool will be of no use at all. High quality is always best when buying hand tools.

In addition to the trowel, a smaller hand tool such as a **small fork, hand fork** or **cultivator**—same tool, different names—can be helpful. A cultivator is handy when fluffing up the surface of the soil in your containers, or sifting out the lumpy bits. I suppose it isn't necessary for gardening in small spaces, but I suspect that once you've gotten used to using it, it will become part of your core tool set.

Cultivator

There are certain characteristics necessary for a tool that will last a long time. All of the same elements that you should look for in a trowel also apply to a cultivator: strong metal that won't bend and is solid from tip to handle, and a comfort grip. Beyond those qualities, there are different styles of cultivators, and you will have to try a few of them out to find what works best for you. I have discovered over the years that a cultivator with bent tines is far more effective than one with straight tines. I can almost guarantee that any cultivator with bent or curved tines is made of a very hard metal that won't bend under regular usage. I have found that cultivators with straight tines are often made of metals that are too soft, and once they're put to the test, even in situations where little force is necessary, the tines bend. Once they've bent once,

it won't take long before they crack and break, and you're left with having to go out and buy a new cultivator. Going with a better quality tool for a little more money up front will probably save you money in the end.

Plastic, fibreglass, wood and steel are only a few of the materials used to make hand tools, sometimes alone and sometimes in combination. I can only speak for myself, but I have had no luck with plastic, regardless of the thickness or weight, nor have I had any luck with fibreglass. And again, I prefer a solid hand tool, rather than a pieced one, whether it is a trowel, dandelion weeder or hoe. They just seem to last longer. I can't emphasize enough that quality is key, and if the new gadgety, kitschy tool on the market just seems too good to be true, then it probably is.

Shovels and **spades** are really only necessary for those who are gardening in the ground or in a raised bed that is in direct contact with the ground. Having a shovel or spade can alleviate some of the bending and kneeling necessary in ground beds. They are good for breaking into hard soil and for adding soil amendments such as compost. Shovels tend to have a bit of a curved blade, which is useful for moving and shifting large quantities of material in one fell swoop, while the blade of a spade is almost flat, with a straight, sharp cutting edge. Spades also have a foothold or tread at the top of the blade on either side of the handle, where you step to push it into the soil.

Regardless of whether it is a shovel or a spade, the blade should be made of a single forged-and-tempered piece of steel, and it should attach to the handle with a closed, reinforced socket and long straps that run up the bottom and top of the handle to reinforce the joint. This is often evident by two bolt heads at different points on the handle. Fibreglass handles are less likely to break when you are using the tool to pry something heavy out of the soil, but a good solid wood handle is fine as well. Try a few out in the store first, and buy what is comfortable and an appropriate length, or you'll find yourself cursing it later on because of a sore back.

Shovel

Spade and pitchfork

A **garden fork** or **pitchfork** tends to be more efficient than a spade at turning over soil and breaking up clumps. Often it is better than a shovel or spade for working in really tough or hard soils. This type of tool is also only necessary for someone with an in-ground or raised bed garden that is in direct contact with the ground. The fork should attach to the handle with a closed socket and straps, similar to shovels and spades.

A **rake** is a necessity for levelling soil in a standard garden bed or raised bed, screening and removing rocks and clumps from the soil surface. There is a wide variety of rakes, but for this purpose, you would want one with solid tines, as compared to a leaf rake that has very flexible tines. A **hoe** is another tool for the in-ground, raised bed gardener. It has a long-handle with a pointed or square blade great for weeding and digging shallow trenches for seeding. For both rakes and hoes, all of the same rules already mentioned apply to the handle and how it's attached, which will ensure a long life for the tool.

Tools for Pruning

Pruners are used for cutting stems and branches up to 1.25 cm thick. There are three types of pruners (also commonly known as shears or secateurs). Bypass pruners, which cut like scissors, make clean cuts and don't crush stems, allowing plants to heal more quickly; anvil pruners, which have a single straight blade that uses a splitting action to cut down on a stem or branch; and ratchet pruners, which are similar to anvil pruners except that they feature a mechanism that cuts in stages and are ideal for people with less hand strength or who have arthritis. Bypass pruners are the most popular, and I highly recommend searching for a pair that has replaceable blades so they can be replaced once they are no longer capable of being sharpened. There is nothing more important, in regard to pruning, than a sharp blade.

Pruners are a necessary tool for any gardener, regardless of what you're cutting. You'll find them indispensable, so it's important to take good care of them. If they get wet, dry them off. A wet blade will become a rusty blade. Keep the blades clean and keep them sharp. If

Pruners

the blade can be sharpened, then sharpen it from time to time; otherwise replace the blades when necessary so you'll always have a clean cut.

If larger pruning jobs are too big for a pair of hand pruners, you might consider buying a good set of **loppers**. They are capable of cutting through branches 5 cm or more in diameter.

Tools for Watering

A **watering can** or a **watering wand** with a **hose** is essential for the success of your garden, whether you're growing tomatoes on your balcony or a wide variety of plants in your raised bed. **Rainbarrels** are great places to fill watering cans and buckets. Even in multi-dwelling environments, often rainbarrels can be set up for residents to use.

Rainbarrel and watering can

Watering cans are made of different materials and come in varied sizes, colours and levels of durability. Certainly if you can find something attractive that will last, then go for it; otherwise purchase something that will stand the test of time, is easy to handle, will not leak and comes with a detachable rose on the spout end so it can be removed for watering jobs that require less finesse.

Watering any type of vertical planter or hanging basket can be difficult depending on its height, size and where it is situated. Is the accessibility adequate or does it require a little strategy and some effort? A watering wand is just the answer for such a situation because it alleviates the need to fill up and then lift a heavy watering can. A watering wand is also ideal for anyone who has lots of plants outdoors because it saves on trips with the watering can. All you need is a hose and a tap.

Watering wand and hose

There are hoses meant for indoor use that attach to the mouth of your kitchen tap, and often they're lightweight, coil for storage and come with a wand so the water is easier to direct into the spots that need it, and because holding up a hose without a wand can be exhausting. This type of hose is perfect for apartment and condo dwellers.

For those gardening in a standard or raised bed, a standard hose is more appropriate. Hoses are available in different materials, ranging wildly in cost, and they come in a variety of lengths. Urban gardeners with limited space can often get away with a 25-foot (7.5 m) hose, or an even shorter one, particularly if they have a watering wand to attach to the end.

Soaker hoses are different from conventional hoses because they are meant to leak, or sweat, leaching water directly into the soil slowly, rather than in a flood. These are ideal for raised beds, and they are incredibly economical and environmentally friendly because you're using much less water than you would with a conventional hose. Using a timer can also reduce the labour of watering a raised bed because you won't even have to turn the water on—the timer does it all for you.

Tools for Supporting Your Plants

Stakes and **supports** are helpful to some plants and necessary for others. For example, tomatoes become rather top heavy once they begin to bear fruit, and tomato cages or stakes will prevent the plants from falling over and risking a broken stem. Trellises, obelisks and staked netting are ideal for plants that produce stems that creep, such as vines. Without the supports, the stems would simply trail downward, which isn't necessarily a tragic result, but one that in some cases may negatively affect the overall appearance of the plant or the fruit produced if left to mature lying in the soil.

As with most other tools and supplies, stakes and supports range dramatically

Soaker hose

Trellis

I am able to reuse my bamboo stakes over and over again from one season to the next because I don't leave them out in the weather year-round, I clean them off once they've served their purpose and I don't overload them; even though they're incredibly strong, they do have their structural limits. Bamboo stakes can be used singly or in groups, such as in a pyramid or tripod form for example, simply by fastening the ends together while spreading the opposite ends apart as feet. This struture can be placed over top of a vine to create a little visual interest as well as function as a support.

in style, form and material. Some supports are made with a certain plant or group of plants in mind, such as a tomato cage. Certainly it could be used for other things, but it was designed to support a tall plant covered in heavily weighted fruit. Sometimes a support can be as simple as a bamboo stake. Bamboo is incredibly strong, super cheap, plentiful and really lasts—if you take care of it.

Some vines and trailing plants can be helped to grow upward by tying them to some form of vertical support. Other plants, such as first-year tree transplants, may need to be tied to stakes for a season. **Biodegradable twine** is made of natural fibres such as jute or cotton. The fibres are softer and gentler to plant stems than synthetics such as nylon or plastic, and natural-fibre twine can be composted when you're finished using it. I find that

Tomato cages

it is also more aesthetically pleasing because it blends into the plant, rather than having the garish colours of synthetics taking attention away from the plant.

Tools for Your Comfort

In just about any gardening space there will be time spent on your knees, and it can be pretty painful without adequate cushion. A **kneepad**, or some other type of cushion, is incredibly important when the only accessible position to your garden, particularly for long periods of time, is on your knees. There are two main types of cushioning: either you can get a pillow-like kneepad that you drop where you want it and then kneel on it, or you can get kneepads that you actually strap onto each knee. Everyone has their preference, so figure out which is yours. Find a good pad, whether it's one you kneel on or the kind you strap on, because it will be used quite frequently and you want it to last.

Gloves are also chosen based on personal preference, and that can depend on level of comfort, durability and how they look. There was a time when I hated wearing gloves in the garden because I just couldn't find pair that fit properly. It wasn't that long ago that the vast majority of gardening gloves were designed strictly with men in mind. The few that were available for women were often flimsy, ill fitting and clearly made for fashion, not function. Today there are heaps of great gloves for men and women, for all hand sizes and job types. The styles range from practical to incredibly well made and comfortable gloves that will truly stand

Gloves

the test of time and abuse. They're available in so many different materials that you really need to try them on to find out what works best for you. My advice is to spend the extra money for a really good pair that you like because a new pair every year or two adds up pretty quickly, and that money would be better spent on new plants.

There are probably other tools and supplies you'll find here and there, things that will either make you more comfortable, make less work of your garden, or speed up the tasks at hand, but the preceding are the essentials, the must-haves for you to end up with great results without a sore back, callused hands and broken nails. The proper tools will just make gardening that much more enjoyable, less strenuous and rewarding, and the small initial investment will more than pay for itself in no time at all.

These containers are ready to be planted up.

Preparing to Plant Your Container Garden

If you're starting out with brand new containers, the main thing is to ensure that there is adequate drainage in the bottom before you start planting. If the containers have already been used previously, they will need to be cleaned. But there are other preparations to make before you start planting. The following sections provide all of the information you need to get your container garden ready to grow.

Container Cleaning

Starting with a clean container is important for minimizing soil-borne plant diseases and for removing deposits from fertilizers and plant root compounds released by the plant into the soil over the previous growing season. Even new containers should be cleaned to remove any dust or various other deposits from transport and handling. Most containers are easily cleaned with mild soap and water and a good rinsing.

Clay pots require a different cleaning process. Soak the containers overnight or longer in a solution of nine parts water to one part bleach. The longer they soak, the easier they are to clean. Use a wire or stiff-bristle plastic brush to give the inside of the container a good scrubbing. Stubborn deposits can be scraped off with a knife or other appropriate scraping tool. Soak the scrubbed container in clean water for 15 minutes to remove the bleach; then give it a quick spray rinse. If you are cleaning glazed containers, make sure the glaze will not be damaged by the bleach.

Potting-mix stains, dirty handprints and general muck can be easily removed from most synthetic materials by simply using a soft cloth and soapy water. A scouring pad may be necessary for tougher stains, but test a small, hidden area first to make sure the pad will not damage the surface of the container.

Container Drainage

If your container does not have adequate drainage, you run the risk of drowning your plants. Some form of opening in the bottom of containers is essential for good drainage. You may need to make extra holes in some containers that do not drain as quickly as needed for the plants you want to grow in them.

Containers that have no drainage, or very minimal drainage, can be used to grow plants that do well in boggy conditions, such as those found along stream banks, ponds and marshes. Decorative containers with no drainage can also be used just as they would indoors, where

If you're worried about soil loss, cover drainage holes with a screen.

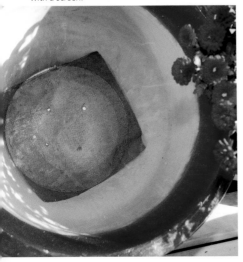

a simple plastic planted pot can be dropped into your decorative pot, but there still needs to be some way for water to drain. Ensure that there is enough space between the two containers. The inside pot should never sit in a pool of water collected between the two pots; otherwise, the rootball of the plant will become waterlogged and begin to rot. This arrangement is only recommended for smaller containers.

Choosing an Appropriate Planting Mix

Most plants need soil that allows excess water to drain away but still retains enough water and nutrients for the plants to use. Commercially available container planting mixes allow good drainage, are lighter weight than garden soils, have nutrient-holding capacity and do not have soil-borne diseases or weed seeds. There is a variety of mixes to choose from depending on what properties your soil needs to have for the plants you want to grow. Try out an organic mix; there has been an increasing number of different organic mixes available on the market over the past five years or so, and they're great to experiment with. You may find that one suits your plant needs better than another, but the only way you'll find out for sure is to try one or two out every season.

Avoid using garden soil in containers because it drains poorly and tends to dry into a solid mass, which can prevent the roots from being able to move and grow and microbes from moving freely around; rot may set in, and the overall

Experiment with different organic mixes to find one that suits you and your plants.

growth of the plant will suffer. You can mix a small amount of good garden soil into your potting soil to add minerals and microorganisms and to improve nutrient-holding capacity, but you may also be introducing soil-borne diseases.

Many commercial planting mixes now contain compost in varying percentages. High-quality compost should be an integral part of every container planting mix. Commercial mixes are also available with water-holding polymers already mixed in, but I am apprehensive to recommend them. Anything synthetic in my potting mixes goes against my organic growing principles, but the polymers can help to maintain moisture in the mix for longer periods—but so can organic amendments such as compost. If moisture retention is a concern, particularly in certain locations such as a direct southern exposure, then I recommend staying away from mixes that are made

up predominantly of peat moss. Peat can hold many times its weight in water, but it also dries out very quickly, and once let to dry out completely, it's difficult to really get moist again, particularly to the core of the rootball. Various amendments will help to improve the density of the mix, which will result in better moisture retention.

Regular commercial planting mixes are mainly peat moss or coir fibre. Coir fibre is made from the husks of coconuts. It is more environmentally friendly than peat moss but can be harder to handle. Mixes may also contain tree bark, vermiculite, perlite, dolomite lime, sterilized loam or clay, superphosphate for quick rooting and often some form of slow-release fertilizer. Just keep in mind that synthetic fertilizers are not organic, and when they're already added to the mix you can't control when the plant is fertilized. I prefer to stay away from these products so I can maintain control over the feeding of my soil and potting mixes, and synthetic fertilizers do have the tendency to be quite harsh, if not fatal, to most microorganisms because they're mostly comprised of salts. Stick with the basics and only feed when necessary, and organically.

Commercially available organic plant mixes are available in different formulations depending on what the manufacturer chooses to use in the product. They are mainly peat moss or coir fibre and may contain high-quality compost, composted leaf mould, bone meal, blood meal, humus, earthworm castings, bird or bat guano, glacial rock dust, dolomite lime, pulverized oyster shells, alfalfa meal, rock dust, rock phosphate, greensand, kelp meal and beneficial mycorrhizal fungi.

If you plan on having a large number of containers, there are large bags and bales of commercial planting mix available. You can also make your own from bulk ingredients to reduce your costs. For the mix I suggest using 40 percent sphagnum peat moss or coir fibre, 40 percent high-quality compost, 10 percent garden loam and 10 percent washed and screened coarse, angular sand. You can add in high-phosphorus guano or bone meal for a root booster and dolomite lime or oyster shells to raise the pH, or you can mix in a commercially formulated organic fertilizer. Add these fertilizer products as instructed on the product label for the volume of soil your containers will hold. A soil test is a useful tool for determining what additions and adjustments your planting mix might need.

Reducing the Weight of Your Containers

Containers can be heavy, but you can take steps to reduce their weight. Do not use gravel in the bottom of the containers, and do not use planting mixes that contain soil or sand. If you have a large container but plan to plant only annuals in it, there is no need to fill the whole container with potting mix; the relatively shallow roots of annuals don't need it. Some of the mix in the bottom half can be replaced with something lighter weight. You can use Styrofoam packing peanuts, broken pieces of Styrofoam packing from goods such as electronic products, well-crushed pieces of newspaper or shredded leaves, or you can use flipped-over plastic pots set in place before the planting mix is added on top. Perennials and shrubs, however, may need all the container space filled with soil for their roots to grow in.

These annuals don't need the entire depth of this container.

Planting Your Container Garden

Generally, you can transplant into containers at the same time you would in a regular garden. There is a proper order to plant into containers. For decorative plants, it is trees first, then shrubs, bulbs, perennials and finally annuals, if in fact you're using more than one type of plant; otherwise it's basically the tallest at the centre and smaller plants on the edges, or tallest at the back cascading down in size to the front. For vegetables and fruiting plants, the formula remains basically the same; put in the largest plants first, then work down in size to the smallest plants.

Fill your cleaned container with moistened planting mix until it is about three-quarters filled. Place the plants into their prospective positions in the container before removing them from the nursery pots to confirm their orientation in the arrangement. Once you've chosen where they're to go, begin working from the middle of the display outward to the pot's edge. After removing the rootballs from the pots or cell packs, gently break the outside of the rootballs apart or score the outer roots with a sharp knife to encourage the roots to spread out rather than continuing to coil into a mass. Place the larger, central focal plants into the container first, followed by the smaller ones. Add more potting mix, as necessary, to surround the rootballs of the plants. Add the smallest and outer-edge plants last, and fill the rest of the container with

planting mix if it settles too much after the first soaking. If you're adding seeds to the mix, then do so at this stage, planting them at the depth recommended on the package. This is also the time to install trellises, stakes and other supports that are needed.

Don't plant too deeply or too shallowly. Use the depth at which that the plants are already growing as a guide for how deeply they should be planted. You don't want to have exposed roots above soil level, but you don't want to bury the crowns, which can lead to rot. An exception to this rule is tomatoes. When planting tomatoes as starter plants, or seedlings, always set them into the soil quite a bit deeper than the level at which they were already growing. The buried stem will produce more roots, which provide more stability for the plant.

How many plants to include in a container is a matter of preference, but overplanted containers look better than sparsely planted containers. The spacing between plants in containers can be reduced from what is recommended on the plant tag. However, too many plants in one container will be forced to compete with each other for space, water, nutrients and light, so you will still need some soil between each plant to provide room for their roots to spread. The more plants in a container, the more often you will have to apply water and fertilizer.

Water plants regularly when they are first planted. Containers can dry out quickly, and new transplants need to become established before they can tolerate adverse conditions.

potting mix, allowing at least 5 cm from the top edge of the pot for watering.

Ensure the soil is without gaps or air pockets in between or under any of the plants. This can be done by gently tapping the bottom of the pot on the floor or by slipping your hand into the potting mix to move the soil into gaps and pockets. Watering will also encourage the potting mix to settle without having to firm it down with your hands. Water until the container is thoroughly soaked. Add more

Planting Trees and Specimen Plants

Ensure that the size of the container is sufficient to allow for root growth, and include enough planting mix to insulate the roots and crown from extreme climate conditions. Trees benefit from having garden loam as part of the planting mix. Garden loam makes the container more stable and gives the tree roots something a little more solid to root into.

Most plants, especially trees, shrubs and perennials, should be planted in spring to early summer to allow them enough time to become established before facing a Canadian winter. This is, of course, if you want to overwinter the hardy plants in the containers. For more on overwintering, see page 103.

The size of container is very important when growing trees and shrubs.

Container Garden Maintenance

Your container garden will need regular maintenance just like a regular garden, but on a much-reduced scale. The most important tasks are watering and feeding. Weeding, grooming, relieving soil compaction and repotting are other tasks that require some attention. You will need a minimal selection of quality tools including a hand trowel, a hand cultivator, a watering can with a diffuser, and bypass hand pruners—or at the very least, a sharp pair of scissors.

Watering

Containers will need to be watered more frequently than plants growing in the ground. The smaller the container, the more often the plants will need watering. Some containers, especially hanging baskets and terracotta containers, may need to be watered twice daily during hot, sunny and/or windy weather. To check if the container needs water, first feel the surface. If it is dry, poke your finger a couple of inches into the planting mix. If it still feels dry, it is time to water. You can also lift the container; if it feels light, it probably needs to be watered.

Water until the water begins to run out the drainage holes.

Water until the entire planting mix is thoroughly soaked and water runs out of the drainage holes.

To save time, money and water, or if you plan to be away from your garden for an extended period, consider installing a drip irrigation system. Drip irrigation systems apply water in a slow, steady trickle, which takes somewhat longer than watering with a watering can or hose but still thoroughly soaks the containers. Drip irrigation reduces the amount of water lost to evaporation. Systems can be fully automated with timers and moisture sensors. This type of system is ideal for raised beds and can be a real money and labour saver. It isn't always an option for container gardens, but it's worth checking into. Consult with your local garden centre or irrigation professionals for more information.

You can lower your watering requirements by adding a thin layer of mulch to each container. Grouping containers together will reduce evaporation from each container. Placing containers in sheltered locations can also reduce evaporation.

Feeding

Plants in containers have limited access to nutrients. Your plants may need a boost during the growing season, and you will have to apply some form of fertilizer. Plants that are heavy feeders will definitely need additional supplements. If you use a good-quality planting mix that has compost and an organic or slow-release fertilizer mixed in, you may not need to add extra fertilizer, but if you do, try to stick with organic, naturally sourced fertilizers. Synthetic fertilizers can be convenient but will kill off all of the critical microorganisms in the potting soil, putting the plants on starvation mode and making them completely dependent on the next feeding. Commercially available fertilizer comes in various forms including liquids, water-soluble powders, slow-release granules or pellets. If you choose to go with a synthetic fertilizer option, follow the package directions carefully.

Your plants may need a boost of fertilizer during the growing season.

The majority of plants will flower most profusely if they have access to enough nutrients. Other plants, such as nasturtiums, grow better without fertilizer and may produce few or no flowers when fertilized excessively. Don't go overboard even with heavy feeders—too much fertilizer, if it doesn't burn the roots, stimulates excessive plant growth and can result in lanky stems and weak or overly lush plant growth that is susceptible to pest and disease problems. Some gardeners fertilize hanging baskets and container gardens every time they water, but they use a very diluted fertilizer so as not to burn the roots.

Healthy soil allows plants to grow better over the course of summer. Organic fertilizers enhance the microorganism population in the planting mix, which in turn makes more nutrients available to the plants. Organic fertilizers don't work as quickly as many synthetic fertilizers, but they often don't leach out as quickly. They can be watered into planting mix or used as a foliar spray as often as weekly.

Organic fertilizers can be simple or complex formulations. They may include alfalfa pellets, compost or compost tea, manure or manure tea, crab meal, coconut meal, corn gluten, kelp meal, sunflower meal, rock phosphate, humus, leaf mould, bone meal, blood meal, earthworm castings, bird or bat guano, dolomite lime, pulverized oyster shells, glacial rock dust, greensand and beneficial mycorrhizal fungi.

Weeding

Weeding your containers isn't often necessary, but when weeds do come up, it is easiest to pull them when they're small. Well-planted containers often exclude enough sunlight at soil level to suppress weed growth. A layer of mulch will also suppress weed growth.

Don't forget about the weeds that pop up around your containers. Pull those ones before they go to seed; otherwise you'll end up with weeds sprouting in your containers.

An assortment of organic fertilizers

Grooming

Good grooming helps keep your container plants healthy and neat, makes them flower more profusely and helps prevent many pest and disease problems. Grooming may include pinching, trimming, deadheading, staking, training vines and climbing plants, and pruning trees and shrubs.

Pinching refers to removing by hand, or with scissors, any straggly growth and the tips of leggy plants. Plants in cell-packs may develop tall and straggly growth in an attempt to get light. Pinch back the long growth when transplanting to encourage bushier growth. Remove any yellow or dying leaves. Pinch back excess growth from more robust plants if they are overwhelming their less vigorous container mates. Keep trailing stems from touching the ground.

If any of your plants, especially annuals, appear tired and withered by midsummer, try trimming them back to encourage a second bloom. Mounding or low-growing annuals, such as petunias, respond well to trimming, as do many herbs such as thyme, oregano and tarragon. Use garden shears and trim back a quarter to half of the plant growth. New growth will sprout, along with a second flush of flowers. Give the plants a light fertilizing as well at this time.

Some plants have very tall growth that cannot be pinched or trimmed. Instead, remove the main shoot after it blooms, and side shoots may develop.

Many annuals and perennials benefit from deadheading (removing faded flowers), which often helps prolong their bloom. It is a good habit to pick off spent flowers when you are checking your

Don't be afraid to trim any plant that is exceeding its boundaries.

Pinching

containers. Deadheading keeps the plants looking their best and prevents your containers from becoming a seed bank, and decaying flowers can harbour pests and diseases. Some plants are self-cleaning or self-grooming, meaning that they drop their faded blossoms on their own. Leaving the seedheads on some plants may provide you with seeds to harvest at the end of the season, either for consumption, such as caraway seeds, or for replanting the next growing season.

Tall plants may require staking or some other form of support. Tie plants loosely to tall, thin stakes with soft ties that won't cut into the plant. Narrow ties are less visible. A great many different types of supports are available these days,

A pretty obelisk dresses up a container and provides support for your plants.

and many of them are quite beautiful. They're made from all sorts of materials, and your choice of which kind to go with should be based on two things: the height of the plant and your own aesthetic. Is your gardening style natural and woodsy? Then maybe a beautiful willow obelisk or branch-like materials that resemble wood are best to support your beans and peas. Or maybe a more contemporary look is what you're going for. There is a great selection of modern and clean-looking, steel or cast-iron supports available. Just make sure to provide a support that can actually support the weight of the plant and provide the height necessary to prevent the plant from flopping over.

Vines in containers can be used as trailers or trained to climb up trellises, netting or other structures. Either the structure is inserted into the container, or the container is placed near the structure. Vines with tendrils climb best on structures that are small enough in diameter for the tendrils to easily wrap around, such as a cage-like trellis or netting. Other climbers will need to be woven through or tied to their structure. Do not be afraid to pinch off any rampant or out-of-bounds growth.

Trees and shrubs will need to be pruned to keep them healthy and in proportion to their container. Each tree or shrub will have its own pruning requirements, such as the best time to prune and how much of the tree or shrub can be removed safely. It is important to learn where, when and how to make proper pruning cuts. There are books that describe proper pruning techniques, and classes on pruning are often offered at horticultural college and university extension programs and public gardens.

Relieving Soil Compaction

Planting mixes in containers can experience soil compaction from the effects of constant watering. A hardened crust can form on the surface that does not allow water and air to penetrate into the planting mix, but it can be broken up easily with a good hand cultivator. Replace the top layer of planting mix in spring.

Repotting Plants

Trees, shrubs and perennials can stay in containers for a number of years with proper care and maintenance. At some point the plants will become rootbound in their containers and will need repotting. Perennials should be divided at this time, and trees and shrubs will need their roots pruned.

Perennials need dividing when flowering is diminished, when the plant loses vigour, when the centre of the plant appears to have died out or when the plant encroaches on other plants in the container. Replant perennial divisions as soon as possible. Extra divisions can be spread around into other containers, shared with friends or composted. Trees and shrubs that need repotting will also appear less vigorous and have reduced flowering.

A common practice for choosing new containers is to move up to the next larger size. Perennials will be divided, so they may not need a larger container.

Trees and shrubs will require a container only a few centimetres wider and deeper than their current container, and they will need some root pruning. Using too large a container can cause overwatering problems.

Tree and shrub containers can be heavy, so keep this in mind when selecting a tree to grow in a small space. Often choosing a smaller specimen is so much easier on the back and the wallet, as well as much easier for overall maintenance. Gently remove the plant from the container and shake out some of the old planting mix. Tease out the larger roots

Perennials in containers will eventually need dividing.

Trees and shrubs in containers will eventually need repotting.

that were encircling the container or growing in toward the centre of the root mass, and cut them off where they would have just touched the edge of the container. Replant the tree or shrub into its new home with fresh planting mix, ensuring it is firmly settled with no air pockets, and give it a good watering.

When tree roots are pruned or damaged, the plant responds by reducing its top growth. Allow the plants to do this naturally; wait and then prune off the dead branches when they become visible, rather than pruning immediately.

Preparing Your Container Garden for Winter

Certainly not every part of Canada experiences cold winter temperatures; however, most areas do. It is important to prepare for winter by performing a few simple maintenance tasks at the end of the growing season. Doing so will prolong the life of your containers and your plants.

Protecting Tender Plants

Tender annuals won't survive winter, but you can help them live well into fall if you protect them from frost. Cover them overnight with sheets, towels, burlap, row covers or even cardboard boxes. Refrain from using plastic because it doesn't retain heat and therefore won't provide your plants with any insulation. If anything, plastic actually traps cold air under the sheeting, which can prove to be a death sentence for your sensitive plants. You can also move your containers to a frost-free area, such as a garage, garden shed or greenhouse. Tender, late-producing vegetables will need to be either covered or placed in a frost-free location on nights with forecasted frost, but put back into a sunny, warm spot during the day for as long into fall as possible.

Some tender perennial plants, such as tropicals, may have to be moved indoors in winter. Tender evergreen plants can be lifted from their container, repotted and brought into the shelter of a greenhouse (if available) or the sunniest, warmest location in your house before the first frost. Most tender plants can be treated as houseplants, whether they return outdoors the following season or not, unless they require a dormant period; woody plants, including trees, shrubs and some herbs and perennials, need to overwinter outdoors where it is cold. Tender plants that require a dormant or cold period during winter are often very difficult to overwinter in containers because there is little protecting the roots; either they will be killed by freeze/thaw cycles, which destroy the cell walls of the plants, or they simply cannot tolerate the extreme cold in your zone. If you're without space to overwinter large, tender plants indoors, cuttings can be taken in late summer and grown as smaller plants for the following spring.

Protect peppers from frost to extend the growing season.

Storing Containers

Containers that will not be used to overwinter plants should be emptied at the end of the growing season and cleaned, disinfected and moved to a suitable storage spot. Containers that have no plants but can't be moved should still be emptied of planting mix, cleaned and disinfected. Inspect all your containers, and if needed, repairs can be done during the winter months. Getting into the habit of emptying, cleaning and disinfecting the containers you are going to reuse the following year will help prolong the life of your containers, even though I know how tempting it is just to leave the contents in the container in fall, either for reuse or to dump after the snow melts. Good gardening habits produce great results, and starting out in spring with clean pots is a good way to put you on the path to gardening success.

Clay containers, especially decorative glazed containers, are particularly subject to winter damage, so if you have paid a premium price for your clay or even stone pots and want them to stand the test of time, you'll need to take extra care with them. If the contents of the container do not need to be overwintered, then it is crucial to remove the potting soil from the pot in fall and then store the container indoors, somewhere that remains above freezing temperatures. Otherwise, any water that has been absorbed by the container over the growing season will expand as it freezes, causing cracks and chipping. If you have no room to store them indoors, the only other alternative is to ensure that your clay and stone containers are completely dry by the time it gets cold enough for them to freeze, reducing or eliminating the risk of cracking from freezing and thawing.

If you are going to try to overwinter plants in a clay or stone pot, the most important thing is to make sure it has a wide opening at the top. When moist soil in the container is subjected to freezing temperatures it will expand, which can crack even the most sturdy clay or stone container. An opening that is equal to or larger than the rest of the container will allow freezing soil to expand upward rather than out.

Insulating Containers

Some plants prefer a cool, moist root environment during the heat of summer, and some plants need extra protection from the effects of winter. Containers can be insulated in similar fashion for both situations. Some materials are better insulators than others. Rot-resistant wood such as cedar makes an attractive container that also offers protection from excessive heating and cooling.

Other containers may need help protecting the roots. One container placed into another with a minimum of 2.5 cm of space between the containers for insulating material such as moistened vermiculite, sawdust or Styrofoam packing peanuts is effective. The inside of a container may be lined with stiff foam insulation for straight-sided containers or lined with a couple of layers of carpet underlay for curved-sided containers. Gardeners in milder zones, such as on

Clay containers should be stored indoors, if possible.

Do not try to overwinter plants in a pot with a narrow opening.

the West Coast, can use a couple of overlapping layers of bubble wrap for insulation.

Overwintering Hardy Plants

When outside temperatures drop below 0° C, the planting mix in containers can freeze solid. Plants continue to use water throughout winter because their dormancy only means their growth rate has slowed, not completely stopped. Frozen planting mix does not allow the plants to take up moisture, and even hardy plants can be killed. Bigger pots are easier for overwintering plants; containers that have a large enough volume of planting mix will increase the chances of the plants surviving winter. Simply put, the more medium surrounding the roots, the more protected they are. This is why plants that are overwintered directly in the ground often have the best chance of survival. When the temperatures begin to warm up, even if it is unusually early in the season, water overwintered plants if they're on the dry side, but only once the planting mix thaws a little.

Some gardeners prefer to keep their hardy plants in containers for only one growing season, then plant them in the ground in fall. Other gardeners simply treat these plants as annuals rather than overwinter them. Another alternative is to leave them in the pots over winter *and* plant them in the ground. This process is known as heeling in, and it's what nursery staff do every winter to overwinter their stock. You simply dig a hole large

enough to accommodate the pot, drop it in and bury it.

Only heel in hardy stock that can tolerate the zone you're in. Just shy of the ground freezing, make sure the rootball is moistened, then dig a hole and drop the whole container in; otherwise the rootball may dry out before it freezes solid. In spring, dig it out, clean it off and voilà, you can put the container right back where you had it. Even people who live in an apartment or condo can often find an approved spot to bury a potted tree, but the key is getting the approval.

The bigger the container, the better the odds for a tree surviving winter.

Overwintering Tender Rhizomes, Bulbs, Corms and Tubers

Perennials that grow from tender rhizomes, bulbs, corms or tubers can be dug up in fall after the top growth dies back, stored over winter and replanted in spring. Dig up the tubers, bulbs, rhizomes or corms before the first hard frost. Shake the loose dirt from the roots and let them dry in a cool, dark place. Once dry, the rest of the soil should brush away. You can dust the roots with an antifungal powder, such as garden sulphur (found at garden centres), before storing them in moistened peat moss or coarse sawdust. Keep them in a cool, dark, dry place that doesn't freeze. Check on them once a month, and lightly spray the storage

Overwinter calla lilies by digging up the bulbs in fall.

medium with water if they appear very dry. If they start to sprout, pot them and keep them in moist soil in a bright window. They should be potted by late winter or early spring so that they will be ready for the outdoors following the last frost. Some gardeners will leave the tubers, etc., in the container and store the whole container inside over winter.

Pests and Diseases in Your Container Garden

Just like any other garden, your container garden may experience occasional attacks from pests and diseases. An infestation need not be a traumatic event, as there are numerous ways of dealing with any problems that arise. As an added bonus, you should not have to worry about soil-borne pests and diseases; they are almost non-existent in container gardens, and even to a certain extent in raised beds, especially when using soil-less planting mixes.

Containers often contain a mixture of different plant species. Because many insects and diseases attack only one species of plant, mixed containers make it difficult for pests and diseases to find their preferred hosts and establish a population. Similarly, annuals are planted each spring, and often different species are grown each year, so again it can be difficult for pests and diseases to find their preferred host plants and establish a population. However, if you grow a lot of one particular annual species, any

Plants in containers are less susceptible to pests and diseases than plants in the ground.

problems that do set in over summer may attack all the plants.

Perennials, trees and shrubs are both an asset and a liability when it comes to pests and diseases. The plants are in the same container for a number of years, and any problems that do develop can become permanent. Yet, if allowed, beneficial insects, birds and other pest-devouring organisms can also develop permanent populations.

Integrated Pest (or Plant) Management (IPM) is a moderate approach for dealing with pests and diseases. The goal of IPM is to reduce pest problems so only negligible damage is done. You must decide what level of damage is acceptable to you. Attempting to totally eradicate pests is a futile endeavour. Consider

Avoid powdery mildew by making sure your plants have enough air circulation.

whether a pest's damage is localized or covers the entire plant. Will the damage kill the plant, or is it only affecting the outward appearance? Can the pest be controlled without chemicals?

IPM includes learning about your plants and the conditions they need for healthy growth. Some plant problems arise as a result of poor maintenance practices. For example, overwatering saps plants of energy and can cause yellowing of the plant from the bottom up. A weak plant is a susceptible plant.

It is also useful to learn what pests might affect your plants, where and when to look for those pests and how to control them. Keep records of any pest damage that occurs because your observations can reveal patterns useful in spotting recurring problems and in planning your maintenance regime.

Prevention and Control

The first line of defence against pests and diseases is to prevent them from attacking in the first place, and the best method of prevention is to provide the conditions necessary for healthy plant growth through the use of cultural controls. Begin by choosing pest-resistant plants. Keep your soil healthy by using plenty of good-quality compost. Spray your plants' foliage with good-quality, fungally dominated compost tea or fish emulsion. A foliar spray acts as a foliar feed and also prevents against fungal diseases. Provide enough space for your plants so that they have good air circulation around them and are not stressed from competing for available resources. Remove plants that are decimated by pests and dispose of diseased foliage and branches. Keep your gardening tools clean

Aphids are pest insects that can cause problems…

and tidy up fallen leaves and dead plant matter in and around your permanently planted containers at the end of every growing season.

Physical controls are generally used to combat insect, bird and mammal problems. An example of such a control is picking pest insects off plants by hand, which is easy if you catch the problem when it is just beginning. Large, slow insects are particularly easy to pick off, and you can squish or rub off colonies of smaller insects with your fingers. Other physical controls include traps, barriers, scarecrows and natural repellents that make a plant taste or smell bad to pests. Garden centres offer a wide array of such devices. Physical control of diseases usually involves removing the infected part or parts of the plant to keep the problem from spreading.

Biological controls make use of populations of natural predators. Birds, spiders, various insects and even certain bacteria help keep pest populations at a manageable level. Encourage these creatures to take up permanent residence in or near your garden, even though it may be difficult on balcony and rooftop gardens. Bird baths and feeders encourage birds to visit your container garden and feed on a wide variety of insect pests. Some beneficial insects are probably already living in or near your garden, and you can encourage them to stay and multiply by planting appropriate food sources. Many beneficial insects eat nectar from flowers.

Chemical controls should be used only as a last resort. Pesticide products can be either organic or synthetic. Organic sprays are no less dangerous than synthetic ones, but they break down into harmless

...but beneficial lady bugs prey on aphids and should be encouraged to live in your garden.

compounds. Try to use organic types, available at most garden centres. The main drawback to any pesticide, whether synthetic or organic, is that it may also kill the beneficial insects you have been trying to attract. Never overuse any pesticide. Follow the manufacturer's instructions carefully and apply no more than the recommended amount. Note that if a particular pest is not listed on the label, that product will not control that pest. Proper and early identification of pests is vital to finding a quick solution.

The Importance of Water Conservation

Conserving water is not only essential for the environment but also for us living in the environment. No water means no plants, and no water or plants means no us. Water is precious, and we're nearing a critical point with the amount of fresh water we have left. We have to become much more conscious of how we use water, and how we can use less of it.

Gardening in any space is an opportunity to be smart with our water usage, and there are simple things we can do to conserve this precious commodity. One of the most economic and easy methods is to use self-watering containers; for more on what they are and how to build your own, refer back to page 64. Another great way to conserve water is to use mulch. We desperately need to get into the habit of making the conservation and preservation of our water sources a priority, and if you do nothing else to save water in your garden, use mulch.

We need to conserve our precious water sources.

Mulch

Mulch is a great way to conserve the moisture in your soil and potting mixes. Most people are familiar with mulching their garden beds, and I do recommend using mulch in any garden bed, including all raised beds. But mulch is also useful in containers. Thick mulch will reduce the amount of evaporation that takes place on a daily basis, resulting in fewer trips with the watering can.

Mulches range in materials, but I prefer ones that will naturally break down, are somewhat fine in texture and won't absorb heat from the sun. Many people use rock as mulch, but it is both harmful and ineffective. Rock absorbs heat and retains it for quite a long period of time, which completely defeats the purpose of mulch. An ideal mulch would stay cool, but at the very least, the mulch shouldn't get any warmer than the surrounding air temperature. The heat from stones, marbles, glass beads or other materials of this type only increases the evaporation rate. Rock mulches are also heavy, which can lead to soil compaction and negatively impact the root systems underneath, and they leave gaps. Gaps allow space for dust and debris to settle, providing the perfect spot for weed seeds to germinate, and if you've ever weeded a rock-covered bed, you'll know how unpleasant it is for the fingers. All of these negative effects can be prevented by staying away from rock and stone mulch altogether.

My favourite mulching material is finely cut bark—not the nuggets, but the finer byproduct leftover from the milling process. It breaks down naturally, is lightweight and inexpensive and can be layered up to 10 cm in thickness to suppress weeds while conserving the moisture content in the soil. A little goes a long way. Bark mulch will also provide organic nutrients to the soil as it breaks down. The odd weed might grow in it, or through it in an in-ground or raised bed, but the material allows for easy removal with no broken fingernails. Bark mulch is perfect for use in containers. And wherever you use it, bark mulch will prolong the gaps between waterings. Once your plants fill in and get bigger, you won't really see the mulch, but where you can see it, it finishes off a well-designed container quite nicely while conserving priceless moisture for your plants.

Using mulch is one of the easiest ways to conserve water.

Bark is one of the best mulching materials.

There are other ways of conserving water, and I encourage you to explore other resources on the subject. There is an incredible amount of information available from people who are creating innovative ways to use less water. It's always worth it to do a little homework. Your plants, the environment and future generations will thank you. A little goes a long way, and every small step we take to be conscious of our water usage adds up to an immense difference in the end.

The Importance of Compost

Sticking with the theme of environmentally friendly gardening, composting is one of many ways of reducing your need to make several trips to the garbage cans in the alley on a weekly basis. It's a great method of recycling and puts back what we take from the environment. There is much to learn about composting in its many forms, but the basics are mostly the same.

Compost is defined as organic matter broken down by bacteria and other organisms, resulting in a dark, soil-like material known as humus. Any organic matter you add to your soil will be of greater benefit if it has been composted first. In forests, meadows or other natural environments, organic debris such as leaves and various other plant bits break down on the soil surface, and the nutrients are gradually made available to the plants that are growing there. In the home garden, where pests and diseases may be a problem and where untidy debris isn't practical, a compost pile or bin creates a controlled environment where organic

Finished compost is of benefit in any garden.

matter can be fully broken down before being introduced to your garden.

Compost is a complete soil amendment, or fertilizer, and is a great regular additive for your garden. Good composting methods will help reduce pest and disease problems. I once read the perfect analogy: just as we are more apt to fight off disease when we are fed adequate nutrition, so are plants more able to fight off pests and diseases when there is adequate nutrition available in the soil. Think of compost as an inoculant for your soil against diseases and pests, if in fact any are present when gardening organically. Compost will also dramatically improve the texture, aeration and drainage of your soil.

The Basics

There are two main types of composting: aerobic and anaerobic. Aerobic composting requires adequate air throughout the pile to provide oxygen for the community of microbes to help move the process of decomposition along. The heat that is given off is a result of the decomposition. Turning the compost will bring oxygen into the mix, so use any method of turning the compost that works for you because oxygen is very important for the process to be efficient. Anaerobic composting is decomposition without air. It is a much slower process, and gases will form, which results in a stinky compost pile that may smell like rotten eggs. This process is often carried out in sealed or closed bins and is not the type of composting you would necessarily find in your neighbour's backyard.

The basis of composting is layering materials in your composter, causing heat to build, which kick-starts the decomposition process, resulting in an earthy, sweet smelling, soil-like material filled with nutrients and beneficial microorganisms. Balance is imperative for composting to be successful and for the microorganisms to thrive. Compost is

These zinnias have benefited from the addition of compost.

only valuable while the materials are in the process of decay, and finished compost is far from complete in this sense. The nutrients in the soil are provided through the process of decomposition. Without this process, microscopic bacteria and other microorganisms wouldn't be able to collect and release the nutrients necessary for plants to thrive. Worms, nematodes, mites and other insects such as sowbugs get up to 60 percent of their protein from the bacteria in the soil because all the bacteria do is consume and release what they've digested before their demise. During this process nutrients are released continually, improving your compost and soil.

Worms are an integral element to the composting equation. Red worms, found only in compost, are different from the earthworms that live in the soil. They are smaller than earthworms but serve a similar purpose. They create air passages

Red worms

for their microorganism neighbours in their common need for an oxygen-rich environment. Red worms migrate into a compost pile when the right elements are in place for them to thrive. The heat produced through decomposition will not kill them, nor will it cause them to leave.

Getting Started

Compost can be purchased from most garden centres, but making it yourself is a relatively simple and rewarding process. There are two ways to go about composting when space is at a premium. You can build or install a small, outdoor composter if you have space in your tiny but respectable yard, or if you have only an indoor or a sheltered outdoor space on your balcony to compost, you too can create black gold for use in your container garden, and it is incredibly easy. It is called vermicomposting, but most people likely know it by the common term: worm composting.

It is helpful, though not necessary, to take a course on composting. There is nothing like hands-on learning to grasp the subtleties of anything, including composting. Everyone has their own methods of making the best compost, and it can become a life-long process to perfect. Once you get into the swing of composting you'll find your own rhythm, but it never hurts to be reminded of the basics. You'll find that the results are totally worth the time invested.

Compost can be made in a pile, a wooden box or a purchased composter. Kitchen scraps, grass clippings and autumn leaves will eventually break down if simply left alone, but as I've mentioned, turning compost will expedite the process exponentially. The process will be most efficient if a few simple guidelines are followed.

There is a wide variety of composters on the market, along with a vast array of

Most urban gardeners will not need a compost bin this large.

Find a composter that works for you.

products to speed up the process. Choose something that works for you. One type of composter may not be ideal for all people. For gardeners with physical limitations or little time, large composters that require a lot of turning with a pitchfork, etc., will not work well. It might be more advantageous to find one that can be easily turned, such as a hollow, ball-like composter that is suspended on a stand and is easily spun with a handle. A plastic garbage bin or other container with holes poked into the sides works nicely as well. You can transfer your kitchen scraps and plant clippings into the container and roll it around on a daily or weekly basis to keep the materials aerated.

Space is another thing to consider; not everyone will have a backyard or patio big enough to house a stand-alone composter, but everyone has space for a worm bin in their home. You may not

be comfortable with the concept of worms in your home, but it's important to understand that the worms aren't casually roaming outside of the bin, and with certain vermicomposters you may never even have to come in contact with the worms. Regardless of your circumstances, take the time to find the right type of composter for your needs.

All composters require adequate drainage. Location can make or break the success of your compost. Choose a location in partial shade, rather than hot sun, where it can drain properly. If animals are a problem in your area, use a cover to prevent them from getting into the compost. If your pile will be directly on the ground, try, if possible, to locate it close to an elm or birch species of tree—the worms seem to like those trees best.

All you need to begin a pile is approximately one cubic metre of material. For composters located directly on the ground, start with larger materials such as twigs to create air pockets at the bottom of the pile. Worms from the soil will find their way into the mix, as will microbes, helping speed up the process. Use brown (dry) as well as green (fresh) materials, with a higher proportion of brown to green matter. Brown matter includes chopped straw, shredded autumn leaves, composted manure, soil, blood meal, nutshells, sawdust and small wood chips, and green matter may be vegetable scraps, grass clippings or pulled weeds. Green matter breaks down quickly and produces nitrogen, which feeds decomposer organisms while they break down brown matter. Be cautious in regions where beech trees grow because the leaves can cause compost to become quite acidic, which isn't necessarily a bad thing for certain plants, but they are in the minority. Keep beech leaves to a minimum in your compost.

Some compostable materials

Egg shells, coffee grounds and filters, tea bags, human and pet hair, feathers, leaf mould, corn cobs, shredded paper and newspaper, and lint from your vacuum cleaner and dryer are all beneficial additions. Coir, which is becoming increasingly popular in Canadian garden centres, can also be added to the composter. It won't add any nutritional content to the end result, but it will lighten the mix somewhat. Kitchen wastes, such as vegetable and fruit waste, should be cut up as small as possible for faster decomposition. It's helpful to run the waste

Add pet hair to your compost, but do not add pet feces.

through the food processor or blender, with a little added water, before adding it to the composter. This will also add moisture to the compost if it's dry.

Do not add dog or cat feces, kitty litter, fats, dairy, meat, bones or anything from the barbecue. These items will begin to smell and will attract pests, resulting in a mess. Do not add anything with pesticides, herbicides or toxic chemicals applied to it, and do not add any non-biodegradable items. Do not put diseased or pest-ridden material into your compost pile, or you risk spreading problems throughout your entire garden. If you do put questionable material in the pile, put it as near the centre as possible, where the temperatures are highest.

Spread the green materials evenly throughout the pile by layering them between brown materials. Layers of soil or finished compost will introduce the organisms necessary to break down the organic matter properly. If the pile seems very dry, add a bit of water as you layer. The pile needs to be moist but not soggy. Adding nitrogen, such as that found in fertilizer, can help speed up the composting process, but avoid the strong concentrations found in synthetic, fast-acting fertilizers, which will kill beneficial organisms. There are ample organic, fast-acting, natural forms of nitrogen to use that will not harm the life in your compost or soil.

The pile can be left to sit and will eventually be ready to use if you are willing to wait several months to a year. To speed up decomposition, aerate the material by turning the pile over or poking holes into it with a pitchfork every few days in the beginning stages, and every week or two once it gets going. In stand-alone, fixed composters, set a pole in the middle of the pile, right to the bottom, and wiggle it around in a circle to allow air to penetrate from the middle outward. It is best to use a rigid tube such as a pipe.

A well-aerated compost pile will generate a lot of heat. Use a thermometer attached to a long probe, like a giant meat thermometer, to take the temperature near the middle of the pile. Compost can easily reach 71° C while decomposing. This heat will destroy weed seeds and kill many damaging soil organisms. Most beneficial organisms are not killed unless the temperature rises above 71° C.

Once your compost pile reaches 71° C, let it sit. If you notice the temperature dropping significantly, turn the pile to aerate it, stimulating the process to start again. When the pile is slow to heat up, try adding a sprinkling of blood meal. A mixture of hoof/horn meal, manure or compost tea also works as a kick-start for heat.

Your compost has reached the end of its cycle when you can no longer recognize the matter that went into it and when the temperature no longer rises when you turn the pile. It may take as little as one month to reach this stage, at which time the compost, rich in nutrients and beneficial organisms, is ready to be added to your soil.

Compost thermometer

Plastic garbage bins work well for anaerobic composting.

Anaerobic Composting

Aerobic composting requires oxygen and heat for decomposition. It also requires regular turning. Anaerobic methods can be ideal for making compost, particularly for anyone who simply does not have the time or space to compost aerobically. Anaerobic composting requires very little effort and can be done by anyone with any amount of space or ability. All you need is a bin to contain the compostable waste, and you're good to go.

Anaerobic composting is done all at once; it works by sealing any collected weeds, clippings, kitchen and household waste in the bin, rather than adding material to a compost heap over time as it becomes available. The materials can still be collected over a short time, but then the bin is sealed. The bacteria work without oxygen, different from the bacteria in open-air compost heaps. Once

the material is composted, you can add it to your potted plants or give it to your friends and family for their gardens.

Method One

- Get your hands on a bin, such as a garbage bin, either plastic or galvanized, but stay away from aluminum—too controversial.
- Choose the location where the bin will sit and try to prepare the bin on site so you don't have to move it later when it is heavy.
- Drill or poke holes into the bottom and sides of the bin (more on the bottom, fewer on the sides), as the bin will require drainage.
- Prepare something for the bin to stand on, such as a short stack of cardboard, newspaper or bricks.
- Sit the material for the stand in a plastic tray large enough to contain

it (drainage trays for planters work well for this purpose and are readily available).

- Place the bin on the stand and begin to fill it with a layer of twigs, straw, fibrous stalks or stems from plants in the garden.
- Cover the bottom layer with 15–20 cm of soil.
- Add layers of shredded green materials and other allowable kitchen and house waste (remember that brown, dry materials hold carbon and green, fresh materials hold nitrogen, so maintain a balance).
- If the mixture is too wet, add sawdust to absorb some of the moisture; to reduce the acidity of the sawdust, add crushed eggshells to the mix.
- Don't pack the layers down, and put the lid on tightly.
- If you're unable to fill the bin all at once, then fill it gradually, but make sure not to leave the lid off any longer than absolutely necessary when you add new material.
- Once all of the layers are complete, leave it alone other than to separate the layers every now and then with a little straw mixed with dry manure or good soil (blood and bone meal or dried chicken pellets will substitute for manure).

Method Two

- Cut out the bottom of a galvanized or plastic garbage bin.
- Place it where it can sit on bare soil in a shady, accessible location. Ensure that it is level and firmly placed on the ground.
- Fill it as you would in Method One, put the lid on and leave it for approximately two months.
- Inspect it occasionally to determine if the contents are sinking and if additional materials should be added (just make sure that you're super quick about it).

Heavy-duty garbage bags can also be used for anaerobic composting.

Vermicomposting

Another option if you're faced with limited space is the vermicomposting method. Vermicomposting, also known as worm composting, takes up little of your time and resources but has so much to offer in a relatively short period of time. This method uses red worms, also called red wigglers, in a bin or container kept indoors throughout the year, particularly in northern climates where the worms will freeze outdoors. The worms are often found at bait shops, your local Master Composter facility or group, or your local environmental resource centre. By simply housing the worms in a rich mixture similar to one in an outdoor composter, the worms will eat their own weight in organic matter on a daily basis. They prefer to be housed in a dark, moist environment such as a box with a lid. In as little as six

Preparing a worm bin (top); adding the worms (bottom)

weeks, the worms will create usable, nutrient-rich compost for your garden.

Some municipalities have their own programs and information available from city departments such as waste management. Along with municipal and grass roots programs and courses, excellent information can be found in our *Composting for Canada* book, as well as at libraries and book stores and from gardening groups. Websites are also a wealth of information; two excellent sites are www.wormcomposting.ca and www.allthingsorganic.com. I'm particularly fond of the Worm Inn Pro offered on the Worm Composting Canada site. It is completely unlike anything I have seen before but works like a charm. It takes up less space than my previous worm bin and allows me to collect the finished product with ease.

A Final Word on Compost

Now that you have the basics for composting, it is helpful to have a short list of things to remember to ensure your success in the process. Keep the following in mind.

- Balance, balance, balance—compost requires balanced quantities of dry and fresh materials combined with manure to encourage decomposition.
- Each layer of material should be no more than 15–20 cm deep.
- A compost heap will thrive if the moisture content is more than 40 percent but less than 60 percent.
- Aeration is necessary for decomposition to occur in a timely manner.
- To achieve aerobic composting, your compost must stand on soil.
- Compost heaps, while in the state of decomposition, should reach an internal temperature of 57°–71° C.
- Use the ratio of 140–200 grams per 1 square metre when using activators such as blood meal or bone meal in your composter.
- Completed compost should be sheltered from weather to protect the content and extend its longevity.

Making compost is easy, good for plants and good for the environment.

The Plants

So now you've found your garden space, and you have good ideas about how to optimize it. The observation process is complete, and you have a detailed record of measurements, sunlight and exposure. You've also worked out what kind of style you're looking for and have an idea of what you want to plant, whether it's vegetables and herbs or an ornate collection of brightly coloured annuals, or any other of the infinite possibilities. But if the possibilities are endless, which plants do you choose?

Edibles

My personal favourite, and one of the most underused groups of plants in small urban settings, is edibles. With the price of produce going up more and more every day, food security should be high up on the priority list of every citizen. With food consistently coming from far away places, and gas prices going up, the time has come to have more control of where and how your food plants came to be. There are heaps of other reasons to take food security to heart, such as food contamination from various bacteria, viruses and pesticides, not to mention reducing the intake and support of genetically modified foods in favour of supporting organically and locally grown food. Each of these issues is critical to our health, the environment and our bottom lines. It doesn't take much effort to make a big difference.

Growing your own edible plants is easy and will save you money at the grocery store.

Vegetables and Fruits

Growing your own fruits and vegetables, wherever possible, even in small quantities, results in less of a dependence on factory farming, big agri-business and big oil companies. It positively impacts the environment because there is no oil or petroleum wasted to transport your produce. It also translates into control—you having control of how your produce is grown and thereby taking more control over your health by putting fresh, organic produce into your body, and if nothing else, your food will taste far better than anything you could ever purchase from a supermarket. Farmers' markets are becoming incredibly popular, and I think it's because people know that the food was grown locally, safely and (in most cases) organically, resulting in pure, rich, genuine flavour. The majority of people who try fresh, local produce would never go back to store-bought produce again.

Homegrown produce has the best flavour.

Growing our own food also forces us to eat more seasonally, which is what our bodies have evolved over time to prefer. Certainly there will be times when we supplement our diets with more diverse food choices from outside of our immediate area. Nothing but root vegetables throughout the winter months would be pretty blah, so produce from the supermarket is a welcome distraction for the taste buds. However, it is still important for more people to grow some of their own food, and there is a wide range of vegetables and fruits that you can grow in an urban setting, even in small spaces, depending on where you live in Canada.

Even if you grow only one vegetable plant, such as a tomato plant, you can reduce your monthly spending on produce throughout an entire growing season by a tidy sum, and you may even have some tomatoes left to ripen into the months of fall. There are tricks to extend the harvest while stretching your dollar. It's quite common now to find mature tomato plants already bearing fruit for sale in garden centres in spring. The plants are usually bearing fruits at all stages, some ripening and others that are only starting to mature, while flowers continue to bloom and produce. If you take one of these plants home, as long as you're pinching outside shoots, fertilizing and keeping the plants evenly moist in a sunny location, you'll have fruit throughout most of the season. Another trick is to select different types of tomatoes that mature at different times, thus extending your season. One variety may be ready for harvest in 57 days, while another will take 70 days or longer. If you start the seed indoors roughly two to six weeks before the last frost, you can transplant older plants at varied stages outdoors immediately after the risk of frost has passed.

With a little planning, it's amazing what an impact you can have on your bottom line. At the time of writing this book, tomatoes were $6.00 for 5 pounds. Depending on how many people are in your household, that 5 pounds may only last you a few days to a week. Just think how much you could save on tomatoes at that price throughout the growing season, which here in Edmonton could last from May to October, if we're lucky. As a vegan I eat a lot of tomatoes, and even though I live on my own, I could save over $100.00 if I grew rather than bought 5 pounds of tomatoes weekly (theoretically at $6.00 for 5 pounds) from May to the middle of October. Granted I would have to have a few plants, probably of varied cultivars, but they would totally sustain my need for tomatoes throughout summer into fall. It's only one tiny example, but just imagine how you could supplement your food supply with other fruits and vegetables.

Vegetables are so easy to grow in containers and raised beds. They do require quite a lot of sun, a little in the way of maintenance and water throughout the growing season, and some time to harvest,

Try growing your own tomatoes.

Vegetables for Partial Shade
- arugula
- beets
- chard
- Chinese cabbage
- kale
- lettuce
- mustard greens
- peas
- radishes
- rutabagas
- scallions (green onions)
- spinach

but the rewards far outweigh the work and time involved. Sun is the one thing that can be hard to come by on a balcony, but I am continually amazed at how much I get from my little balcony garden, and it tastes so good! And the more vegetables you grow, the more proficient you become at it.

Growing fruit in urban spaces, particularly small spaces, is a bit different. Often full sun is necessary for fruit production, as is a dormant period for perennial or woody fruiting plants such as gooseberries, and sometimes the yield can be quite low with only one or two plants. That being said, I still think fruit is worthy of experimentation to determine if you can coax your plants to produce enough for you and your family. Sometimes having fresh strawberries straight from the plant over a period of four weeks is enough to satisfy the palate and the bottom line.

Fruits for Partial Shade
- alpine strawberries
- blackberries
- blueberries
- currants
- gooseberries

Herbs

Herbs are quite common in urban gardens because we've grown accustomed to growing them in containers, on windowsills and in other small spaces. Herbs can be mixed with other plants in small gardens or containers, or they can be grown in a larger grouping. There are literally thousands of herbs to grow, and I'd hate to see anyone limit themselves to nothing but basil, rosemary and thyme. If you don't believe me, check out the Richters catalogue. Based in Goodwood,

Strawberries will grow quite well in a container.

Thyme is a yummy filler plant for a container.

my balcony, cut a fresh bunch of parsley and be eating tabouli 10 minutes later. And cutting a bunch of stems only encourages the plant to produce more. Many times I've been able to bring the plant indoors just before a hard frost, thus providing myself with parsley for a few more months even though the growing season is over outdoors. I have friends who have a similar relationship with basil because they're crazy for pesto, while others who barbecue a lot love having fresh herbs for rubs and marinades. You just can't beat fresh herbs.

I firmly believe that any way of supplementing our diets with organic, fresh food, even herbs, is paramount to a healthy lifestyle. It takes only a little to make a huge difference. Grow herbs if for nothing else but the enjoyment it brings when preparing meals and consuming the results.

When considering which herbs to grow, note that there are annual and

Ontario, Richters has a superb selection of herbs beyond anything you could have imagined.

There may be one herb you just can't get enough of—parsley, for example. Fresh parsley can be expensive to buy, but it is incredibly inexpensive, and easy, to grow at home. There are so many ways to enjoy parsley, and to have an unending supply right out your door is not only convenient but also one hundred times more flavourful than store-bought. I like to make tabouli throughout the growing season because I can make it entirely from plants in my garden, and parsley is one of the main ingredients. It's so satisfying to go onto

Parsley is easy to grow at home.

perennial herbs. Some can live year-round and others have a very short life. Some will benefit from being cut and used on a regular basis while others will take much longer to regenerate growth, if they do at all. There are herbs that thrive in full sun and others that prefer a more protected, shaded area. Always do your homework first, and if you're still unsure, or if you come across something interesting but unfamiliar at the garden centre, ask the staff for tips and information. You may have made a discovery that can improve both your gardening and your culinary experience.

Herbs for Partial Shade

- chives
- mint
- parsley
- sorrel

Annuals

Annuals, or bedding plants, are often the first type of plants people consider for small urban spaces, particularly when those spaces are mostly made up of containers and decorative pots. Certainly there is nothing wrong with annuals, and in many ways they make sense. Often people only want the plants to grow throughout the growing season, for colour, to soften hard edges and as an accessory for their home, like accent cushions on a couch. Condo and apartment dwellers aren't usually looking for plants to overwinter, and for good reason—it can be a lot of work. Overwintering is not impossible, but it takes time, skill and some finesse. Success with overwintering also depends on where in Canada you are gardening. The bottom line is that annuals are easy; with minimal maintenance, they're beautiful for the growing

Pretty annuals come in almost any colour.

Annuals can be expensive, so try to stick to your list at the garden centre.

perfect amount of water, light and synthetic fertilizer until they are sold. Growth retardants are sometimes used to keep the young plants stocky and full. When they're ready for sale at the garden centre, the plants have been basically forced to produce huge quantities of blooms while they stay short and dense. Once out of that environment, many of those annuals tend to slow down to a more normal or average rate of flower production, and the growth retardants wear off, resulting in taller, thinner plants that look spent in a relatively short amount of time. Granted this scenario isn't always the case, but it is very common.

It's also very common now to find one single annual plant for sale in a container such as the ever-popular 10 cm pot. There was a time when you could get six petunias in a cell-pack, all of them ready to produce but not monsters fighting to get out of those packs, for roughly $1.50. Now it's customary to find one single petunia, albeit older, fuller and covered in flowers, for five or more times that price. Even annuals in cell-packs are bigger, older and far more expensive than they used to be.

season, and once it gets cooler in fall, it's time to let them go. No commitments.

Annuals used to be really inexpensive, but not so long ago, the price began to go up. The majority of annuals are sold as started plants in cell-packs, undivided trays or small pots. The seeds or cuttings are started at a large growing operation, usually far away from where you actually buy the plants, and are then sent to garden centres as tiny seedlings often referred to as plugs. Garden centre staff transplant the plugs into trays or cell-packs. Those plugs have been and will continue to be meticulously cared for in a controlled environment with perfectly monitored temperatures and humidity and the

When you're shopping for annuals, look around for low prices and try to stick to your list. Don't go overboard. It is very easy to get drawn into all of the colours, textures and varieties, but you only have so much space. Also, there are supplies you'll need other than the plants, especially if you're a beginner, so you don't want to blow your whole budget on plants. You're bound to find good prices for good plants if you just look around a bit.

You might think I'm poo-pooing annuals and the way they're frequently grown commercially these days. I may not agree with the method entirely, but I still buy a few annuals from garden centres every year rather than starting them from seed myself because it takes time and space to start plants well, and I have very little time or space, as do most people who are reading this book right now. When we buy well-started annuals we tend to pay for the convenience aspect, and as busy as most of us are these days, it's often worth it. I can take them home and plant them up, and the resulting container looks completely filled out. It's like an instant garden.

So there are pros and cons to annuals. If you have space for only one container, and you'd prefer it to be filled with colour and texture for maximum impact, then annuals fit the bill. I prefer to have a balance of everything myself, a pop of colour here and there but more of an edible garden on my balcony, to stretch my food dollar and control how some of my food is grown. Every person will have different tastes, however, and there is nothing wrong with that.

Even in a small space you can have a mix of a colourful annuals and delicious edibles.

Perennials

Perennials are another group of plants to consider for small urban spaces. Perennials can be grown in small spaces surrounded by nothing but hardscapes, but depending on where you are in Canada, they can be more challenging in regions with reliably cold, if not extreme, winter temperatures.

Perennials should be chosen on the same basis as any other plant, including light, space, moisture and exposure requirements. What will be different than annuals, however, is choosing them based on whether or not they will survive winter in a container in your area. In the ground, perennials have ample root protection, but in any type of container, even a large one, the roots have less surrounding protection. This lack of protection can be a deal-breaker for a perennial. Because there is less medium surrounding the roots, the plant will inevitably go

The perennials in this container will be a challenge to overwinter.

through freeze and thaw cycles throughout winter. As the roots freeze and thaw, the cells in the roots basically break down and fail. If there is nothing to draw up moisture and nutrients, the plant will die. It's a tricky process to overwinter perennials in containers outdoors in cold regions, particularly zones 4 and colder. You have to ensure they remain frozen and moist without being too wet, on par with what the ground is doing. There is a pretty high failure rate and it requires some experimentation to determine what works for you, but overwintering perennials in containers is not impossible.

Too much cold is not good for perennials, but neither is too much warmth. Bringing potted perennials into the house, or any place that is too warm, just simply won't work. Even outside in warmer parts of the country, certain perennials may not get enough of a cold period for a proper dormancy, which exhausts the plants over time and ultimately shortens their life. The vast majority of perennials require long periods of cold to go into dormancy, and without that rest they continue to grow at an active rate. Eventually the plant will run out of steam, resulting in spindly stems and leaves, fading, reduced flowering or no flowering at all. The plant will look more and more spent, ultimately dying. With perennial prices being what they are, perennials are not often worth the risk or work involved in keeping them alive.

This all being said, if you're hooked on the idea of perennials in your urban setting, namely containers, then go for it. Just remember that there may be casualties—it's nothing you did or didn't do, it's just the way it works. Enjoy the plants for the season or two that you have them and then start fresh. The other alternative is to enjoy the perennials for a summer and then give them to someone with an in-ground garden. Even planted in late fall, the perennials will likely survive and live a long life. It's a win-win situation, allowing you to have a diverse variety of plants in your containers while your gardening friends benefit from them in years to come. You could even split the cost. And if you're anything like me, planting the same things in my containers year after year is boring, so starting from scratch the following spring is exciting, and I'm happy to give my perennial plants away at the end of the season.

Overwinter your lilies by digging up and bringing in the bulbs.

Trees and Shrubs

Maybe you don't want any flowering plants at all. Maybe you want to make a statement. Maybe the space you have is more vertical than horizontal. Trees and shrubs are an option to consider, and the selection is widely varied.

Regardless of the species, the most important consideration regarding trees and shrubs is placement. Almost all of these plants require a dormant period, so ultimately the best location for any tree or shrub is in a plot in the ground, like the front or back of a townhouse would have. This way the tree or shrub

has the ground to protect its roots from freeze/thaw cycles. If you're going to plant a tree or shrub in a container on a balcony or patio, placement of the container is very important. The container would have to be quite large, particularly when planting for the purpose of overwintering. But with size comes weight and less of a chance to move the container to a more protected spot throughout the winter months. Planting a tree or shrub in the right place will give it the best chance of surviving winter.

It is also important to place a tree or shrub where it has space to grow. Adequate space is paramount to even the smallest tree or shrub. Over time, if you're able to overwinter it, it will grow to a mature specimen. It simply is not an option to continually prune a woody ornamental down to size year after year. You must choose a specimen that fits the space you have. There is a reasonable selection of dwarf species available, both in trees and shrubs. Every year, with space at an ever-increasing premium, more and more varieties are bred for small spaces. All you have to do is look for them.

Make sure your tree has enough space to grow.

Tropicals

Tropicals are another group of plants that is well-suited to small urban spaces. Often they're forgotten as candidates for outdoor use, but they can be mixed in with other groups of plants or left on their own as specimens. As a bonus, you can take tropicals indoors for the colder months, prolonging their life and your enjoyment of them.

Tropical plants, or what some people know as houseplants, require all of the usual considerations such as light, space and exposure tolerance and needs. Most tropical plants are best suited to high light locations because of where they originated, but there are others that cannot tolerate extreme heat, direct sun or low humidity levels. Some tropical plants flower, and some don't. They come in just about every size, colour and texture, and they can provide whatever look you're searching for. For example, height and impact may be on your list, and many tall, leafy tropicals can provide the vertical element you're looking for without taking up space from side to side.

There are also trailing or creeping tropical plants ideal for the edge of containers and hanging baskets. More and more garden centres and nurseries are providing tropicals as basket stuffers, but the plants are sold as annuals without people even taking notice. It's refreshing to see this trend grow season after season, but a little disappointing to see the tropicals lumped into the annual category because customers may not know that they could repot their tropical plants to take inside during winter, then use them again year after year. It is rather wasteful to just throw them away, unknowingly or not, but it's still nice to have the variety.

Bougainvillea is a pretty tropical that can be grown as a houseplant.

The Top Threes

In each grouping of plants, there are the best and worst for every growing condition and space. The following are some of the best for small, challenging urban spaces, particularly for container gardening, based on ease of growth, maintenance and harvest. They are not no-fail suggestions, but they are the most popular plants you'll see growing in these types of spaces, and for good reason: they work.

Never be afraid to think outside the box. These plants are just the tip of the iceberg, and if you're a beginner and are leery to venture off into unfamiliar territory without a firm recommendation, then these are the ones to start with. I suspect that in time you'll find yourself feeling more and more confident about trying new plants in new configurations and starting trends no one else has thought of. Remember that you cannot fail, but rather always learn. Remind yourself regularly that gardening is meant to be fun and rewarding, and you'll have a lifetime of gardening successes.

Beans

Phaseolus, Vicia

This incredibly diverse group of legumes is sure to please everyone; there are few things as delicious as fresh beans for dinner, straight out of the garden. Most people are familiar with the string bean, but there is so much more to this group of vegetables. The selection is almost endless.

Starting

Beans are quite possibly one of the easiest plants to grow from seed. The seeds are large and easy to handle, and they sprout quickly in warm, moist soil. Plant them directly in the garden after the last frost date has passed and the soil has warmed up. They can be planted 10–20 cm apart.

Growing

Beans grow best in **full sun**, but they tolerate some light afternoon shade. The potting mix or soil should be of **average fertility** and **well drained**. Bush beans are self-supporting, but climbing beans need a pole or trellis to grow up. The support structure should be in place at planting time to avoid disturbing the young plants or damaging their roots.

Bush beans can become less productive and look unattractive as summer wears on. Pull them up and plant something else in their place, or plant them with companions that mature more slowly to fill in the space left by the faded bean plants.

Harvesting

The most important thing to remember when harvesting beans is to do so only when the foliage is dry. Touching wet foliage encourages the spread of disease.

Different types of beans should be picked at different stages in their development. Green, runner, wax or snap beans are picked once the pod is a good size but still young and tender. As they mature, they become stringy, woody and dry. Beans that are eaten as immature seeds should be picked when the pods are full and the seeds are fleshy and moist.

Beans for drying should be left to mature on the plant. Once the plant begins to die back and before the seedpods open, cut the entire plant off at ground level, leaving the nitrogen-fixing roots to enrich the soil, and hang it upside down indoors to finish drying. You can then remove the beans from the pods and store them in airtight containers in a cool, dry place. The beans will keep for 10 to 12 months.

Tips

Beans are very ornamental, with attractive leaves and plentiful flowers. Climbing beans can be grown up fences, trellises, obelisks and poles to create a screen or feature planting. Bush beans can be used to make low, temporary hedges or can be planted in small groups in a border.

Climbing beans are popular among gardeners with limited space because you can get more beans for less space.

Recommended

P. coccineus (runner bean) is a vigorous climbing plant with red or sometimes white or bicoloured flowers. 'Scarlet Runner' has bright red flowers and is one of the best and best-known cultivars. The beans can be eaten with the pod when they are young and tender, or the plants can be left to mature and the pink-and-purple-spotted beans can be dried. Plants produce edible beans in 70 days but need about 100 days for dry beans. 'Pantheon' is another stringless selection. It is ready in 75 days and has flat, juicy pods 2.5 cm wide and 25 cm long.

P. lunatus (lima bean) may be climbing or bush, depending on the cultivar. The

beans are eaten as immature seeds and should be picked when the pods are plump but the seeds are still tender. They take 70 to 85 days to mature. 'Fordhook' is a popular bush variety, and 'King of the Garden' is a good climbing selection.

P. vulgaris (wax bean, green bean, bush bean, pole bean, snap bean, dry bean) is probably the largest group of beans. Some of them are eaten immature in the pod, and others are grown to maturity and used as dry beans. Bush bean cultivars may be yellow, such as 'Gold Rush' and 'Sunburst'; green, such as 'Ambra' and 'Stallion'; or purple-podded, such as

'Royal Burgundy.' Purple beans turn bright green when cooked. Bush beans take 50 to 60 days to mature.

Pole beans, such as 'Blue Lake' and 'Kentucky Blue,' take 50 to 55 days to mature. 'Bush Blue Lake' is a dwarf bush selection with dark bluish, 15–16 cm long beans that are good for canning, freezing or eating fresh.

Dry beans are usually bush plants and take about 100 days to mature. They include kidney, pinto and navy beans. A popular selection for home growers is the red-and-white-spotted 'Jacob's Cattle.' 'Red Noodle' produces beans that are

red-burgundy in colour and reach lengths of 40–50 cm. They're produced in clusters and are sweet in taste. The colour fades when cooked, but they're good enough to eat fresh.

Shell beans (wren's eggs, horticultural beans, bird eggs, speckled cranberries, October beans) come in both pole and dwarf varieties and can produce big harvests in small gardens. Most beans can be used as shell (or shelling) beans, which have the pods removed before they are cooked or dried. The colourful, mottled pods can be eaten like snap beans when young, but most people use the rich, nutty, red-speckled seeds, which mature in 65 to 70 days, as fresh shell beans and for canning and freezing. One selection that is highly coveted for shell bean use is **'Supremo,'** which is ready for harvest in 85 days.

V. faba (broad bean, fava bean) **'Sweet Lorane'** has great flavour and cold hardiness. It is ready for harvest in 90 to 140 days. It produces fragrant flowers followed by tough-skinned pods. They must be soaked overnight before using. **'Windsor'** grows 90 cm–1.2 m tall and produces pods 12–20 cm long, containing 5 to 7 beans. These wonderfully thick broad beans are mature in 4 to 5 months and shell very easily.

Legumes (including beans) are known for being able to fix nitrogen from the air into the soil through a symbiotic relationship with bacteria, which attach to the roots as small nodules. The bacteria turn the nitrogen from the air into useable nitrogen for the plant; in return, the plant feeds and supports the bacteria. The bacteria are present in most soils and are also available for purchase as a soil inoculant. Some bean seeds are also pre-treated with the bacteria.

Problems and Pests

Pick beans only when plants are dry to reduce the spread of disease. Problems with leaf spot, bacterial blight, rust, bean beetles and aphids can occur. Disease-infected plants should be destroyed, not composted, once you've harvested what you can.

Kale, Collards & Mustard Greens

Brassica

These nutrient-packed, leafy cabbage siblings are some of the most decorative members of the Brassica family. This grouping is growing steadily in popularity, and for good reason; the flavour, texture and pure versatility are second to none. Collectively, this group is incredibly nutritious as well as delicious and is not just a garnish anymore.

Starting

All three of these plants can be sown directly into the garden. They are all quite cold hardy and can be planted pretty much as soon as the soil can be worked in spring. A light frost won't harm them, though you should cover the young plants if nighttime temperatures are expected to drop to -10° C or lower. You may wish to make several successive plantings of mustard because the leaves have the best flavour when they are young and tender.

Growing

These plants grow best in **full sun**. The potting mix or soil should be **fertile, moist** and **well drained**. Mustard in particular should not be allowed to dry out, or the leaves may develop a bitter flavour.

Harvesting

Because the leaves are what you will be eating, you don't have to wait very long after planting to start harvesting. Once plants are established, you can start harvesting leaves as needed.

The leaves may become tough and bitter if they get too large or start to turn yellow. To extend the harvest, pick only what you will use on a daily basis, and select the largest leaves first. Frequent, small harvests will provide you with fresh, flavourful leaves for weeks to come.

Kale

Tips

These plants make a striking addition to beds, borders and mixed containers, where their striking foliage creates a good complement and backdrop for plants with brightly coloured flowers.

Recommended

B. oleracea var. *acephala* (collards; Scotch kale, curly-leaved kale) and *B. oleracea* var. *fimbriata* (Siberian kale, Russian kale) are the kales and collards; however, the two common names are not always used consistently.

Popular kale selections include the following. **'Blue Curled'** and **'Blue Ridge'** have good flavour and vigour. **'Improved Dwarf Siberian'** is ready in 50 days, maintaining its quality in the garden long after other selections have bolted. **'Curly Green'** is as it's named—very curly, green and great even when flowering. **'Tuscan'** ('Black Tuscany,' 'Lacinato,' 'Dinosaur') is one of the tastiest forms of kale and is beautiful as an ornamental as well. It bears long, strap-like, blistered, dark green to almost black leaves.

Popular collards include **'Green Glaze,'** often referred to as "greasy greens." **'Flash'** is an early variety with smooth leaves. This selection is very slow to bolt and will continue to produce while the leaves are picked throughout the season. **'Hi-Crop'** has crinkled, blue-green, smooth leaves and a sweet flavour. This bolt-resistant variety is ready in 70 days.

B. juncea subsp. *rugosa* (mustard) forms large clumps of ruffled, creased or wrinkled leaves in shades of green, blue-green, bronze or purple. **'Savanna'** produces large, thick, deep green leaves with a savoury but mild flavour. **'Mizuna'** ('Japonica') is a Japanese mustard variety with finely cut, curled leaves with a pleasant, mild flavour. Ready in 65 days, this selection will continue to grow after being cut. **'Red Giant'** produces brilliant maroon leaves with light green midribs. The leaves are spicy and flavourful and ready for harvest in 45 days.

Problems and Pests

Problems with cutworms, leaf miners, caterpillars, root maggots, cabbage white butterfly larvae, white rust, downy mildew and powdery mildew can occur.

Mustard greens (above); collards (below)

Potatoes

Solanum

Potatoes were cultivated in South America for centuries before they were introduced to Europe by the Spanish. They were only introduced to North America after European immigrants brought them here. Today, heirloom varieties are in fashion, mixing it up with newer cultivars fancy and plain, small and large; no matter what new varieties come out, the heirloom potatoes are often the best and have stood the test of time.

Starting

Sets of seed potatoes (small tubers) can be purchased and planted in spring a few weeks before the last frost date, as long as the soil isn't too cold and wet. Young plants can tolerate a light frost, but not a hard freeze. The seed potatoes can be cut into smaller pieces, as long as each one has an "eye," the dimpled spot from which the plant and roots grow. Each piece needs 30–45 cm of space around it to grow.

Growing

Potatoes prefer **full sun** but tolerate some shade. The potting mix or soil should be **fertile, humus rich, acidic, moist** and **well drained**, though potatoes adapt to most growing conditions and tolerate both hot and cold weather. Mound soil up around the plants to keep the tubers out of the light as they develop.

Harvesting

The tubers begin to form around the same time the plants begin to flower, usually sometime in midsummer. You can dig up a few tubers at a time from this point on as you need them.

The remaining crop should be dug up in fall once the plants have withered, but before the first hard frost. Let them dry for a few hours on the soil, and then brush the dirt off and store the potatoes in a cold, dark place. You can even save a few of the smaller tubers for planting the following spring.

Tips

When grown in containers, make sure that the depth is adequate for the tubers to grow and to allow for mounding the soil up as the tubers mature. Decorative tall, cylindrical planters are fine, but containers designed specifically for growing potatoes are best. Often they are collapsible (see page 40), but potato containers can also be made at home from items around the house, such as a large garbage can. See next page for how.

Recommended

S. tuberosum is a bushy, mound-forming plant. It bears tiny, exotic-looking, white, pink or light purple flowers in mid to late summer. There are many varieties of potatoes. They can have rough or smooth, white, yellow, brown, red or blue skin and white, yellow, purple or blue flesh. A few popular varieties include **'All-Blue,'** with smooth, blue skin and light purple-blue flesh; **'Norland,'** with smooth, red skin and white flesh; and **'Yukon Gold,'** with smooth, light beige skin and yellow flesh.

Beyond the more traditional, well-known varieties are some of the more unusual and fun ones. **'Chaleur'** is a high-yielding, early Canadian variety with great tolerance to hot and dry conditions and bears large tubers. **'Kennebec'** is slowly on its way to becoming a commonly known spud because of its high yield potential of oblong tubers and its disease and drought tolerance. **'Banana'** is a fingerling type with yellow skin and flesh. Its vigorous growth results in heavy yields. **'Purple Peruvian'** is also a fingerling, but it is purple inside and out.

Problems and Pests

Potatoes are susceptible to a variety of diseases, including scab. Avoid planting them in the same spot two years in a row. Potato beetle is the most troublesome insect pest.

'Kennebec'

How to build a potato planter out of a standard garbage can:

This is a great project for those of you living in an apartment because it will allow you to grow potatoes on your balcony. Decorative containers often aren't tall enough to accommodate the depth necessary to grow potatoes. This method is super easy and inexpensive, and the finished product is very easy to work with and to harvest from.

Supplies

- one standard galvanized or plastic garbage can (approximately 32 gallon size)
- a drill or a hammer and a strong, long, wide gauge nail
- potting soil (enough to fill garbage can ⅔ full)
- a drainage tray large enough to accomodate the garbage can (option #1 for drainage) **or** 2" x 4" lumber cut into two 24" lengths (option #2 for drainage)
- seed potatoes (about 6–12 should do)

All parts of the potato plant are poisonous except the tubers, and they can become poisonous if they are exposed to light. Green flesh is a good indication that your potatoes have been exposed to light. To protect your potatoes, mound soil around the plants, 2.5 cm or so per week, from midsummer to fall. A straw mulch also effectively shades the developing tubers. Use mulch in containers if necessary.

Purchase seed sets of a variety that interests you rather than trying to grow potatoes bought from the grocery store. Potatoes from the store may have been treated to prevent sprouting, or they may be poorly suited to grow where you live.

Put it Together and Grow

- Cut your seed potatoes into quarters, making sure to have at least one eye per piece. Let them sit out overnight to dry.

- Drill or pound holes into the bottom of the garbage can for drainage. Six to eight holes should do, but more is better.

- Select a sunny location for the garbage can to sit. Set your drainage tray down and place the can into the tray. Or, if you've chosen the boards, set them down parallel to one another and approximately 18" (45 cm) apart, and place the garbage can on top of the boards. Make sure the can is balanced and stable.

- Fill the garbage can with approximately 6–8" (15–20 cm) of potting mix. Place the pieces of seed potato cut side down into the soil and cover with 3–4" (7–10 cm) of potting mix. Water thoroughly, covering all of the soil surface area, until you see the water trickle out of the bottom.

- Keep the soil just moist until the sprouts emerge through the surface. Once the plants are approximately 6" (15 cm) tall, cover them up so only ⅓ of the stem is sticking out of the potting mix. Continue to follow this process until the plants begin to flower. Fertilize once or twice with a natural, organic fertilizer.

- Continue to keep the potting mix just slightly moist while the plants are flowering and for a week or two afterward. Then stop watering and let the plants dry out.

- Once the plants have withered, allow the potatoes to cure in the soil for a few more weeks if you're planning on storing them for any length of time. If you plan on using the potatoes right after harvest, then you can forgo the curing process. Retrieve the potatoes a few at a time by digging into the can with a trowel or your hands, or just dump everything out to harvest all of the potatoes at once.

Is your potato high or low in starch? To find out, cut one in half, rub the cut surfaces together and then stick them to one another, like you were putting them back together. If they stick, the starch content is high. High-starch varieties are best for baking and mashing. Low-starch spuds are best for boiling and for potato salad.

Blackberries

Rubus

Blackberries and raspberries share the same genus but are different species. The biggest difference between the two, aside from colour, is that the "core" of a blackberry remains in the berry when picked, whereas the core of a raspberry breaks free when picked, resulting in a hollow berry. Another difference is the flavour. Blackberries have a mild flavour, while raspberries are quite tart.

Blackberries are classified by their growth pattern as either trailing, semi-erect or erect.

Starting

Blackberry plants are available as transplants from the nursery or garden centre. Plant out potted blackberries once the risk of frost has passed and the plants have been hardened off.

Growing

Blackberries prefer **full sun**. The soil or potting mix should be **light to medium, sandy** and **well drained**. Blackberries are very drought tolerant and do not like to sit in wet, heavy soils. They are known to grow in nutritionally poor soils.

Blackberries produce thorny canes. The root system is considered to be perennial, but each shoot is biennial, meaning that each of those shoots will only live for two years. In the first year a cane will reach its mature height, and in the second hear it produces fruit but dies soon afterward. Cut out the dead canes from year to year.

Blackberries are hardy in certain parts of Canada, but not below zone 4, particularly in containers. To overwinter blackberries, either bury the pots in the ground in fall and dig them up in spring when the ground thaws, or store them in an area that is cold enough for the root-balls to remain frozen without the threat of going through a number of freeze/thaw cycles. Make sure the bushes remain moist, but not too wet, throughout the winter months. Take the containers back out when it's safe to do so in spring. When overwintered from one year to the next, blackberries will need to be repotted into larger containers every few years, depending on their growth rate.

Harvesting

Blackberries are best left on the plant until they're completely ripe; hold off on picking them until the berries turn dark and full. As with any berries, you'll have to pick almost daily as the blackberries mature. Ensure that the white middle "plug" in the centre of the berry does not detach while picking. If you find that the berries are separating while picking, cut the berry stems with clippers or scissors. Try not to handle the berries any more than necessary, as they are easily damaged.

Once picked, store the berries in a cool location. Blackberries can be eaten fresh or frozen, or used in baking, salads, sauces and desserts.

Tips

This fruiting shrub can grow quite tall in one growing season, and it is known to be incredibly invasive. Blackberries produce suckers, or shoots, and this is how they spread into masses of thorny canes. They are ideally suited to urban spaces because they will remain contained in a raised bed or container.

Recommended

R. fruticosa forms a thicket of thorny stems or canes. Canes grow up to 3 m tall and can spread 1.5 m or more. White or pink, late-spring or early-summer flowers are followed by red or black berries in late summer. A wide variety of cultivars is available for zones 5 and higher, such as 'Chester Thornless' and 'Illini Hardy.' These erect-spring types are ideally suited to gardens in Ontario and in the lower mainland of BC. 'Doyle's Thornless' is a patented blackberry that claims to be hardy to zone 3, but heavy mulching is recommended once the container is buried in the ground for the colder months. (Zones 4–8)

Problems and Pests

Blackberries can be targeted by aphids, leafhoppers and leafrollers. Cane blight, anthracnose and crown gall can also be problematic.

Blueberries

Vaccinium

These attractive bushes can be low and spreading or rounded and upright. The leaves turn a beautiful shade of red in fall. Blueberries are well suited to growing in small, challenging urban spaces, with the added asset of delicious summer fruit.

Starting

Plants can be purchased and planted at any time, but the earlier they're planted in containers, the sooner you'll have fruit.

Growing

Blueberries grow well in **full sun, partial shade** or **light shade**. The potting mix or soil should be of **average fertility, acidic, moist** and **well drained**. Blueberries grow best in an acidic mix that is peaty or sandy. The soil can be amended with an acidic fertilizer.

To overwinter blueberries, either bury the pots in the ground in fall and dig them up in spring when the ground thaws, or store them in an area that is cold enough for the rootballs to remain frozen without the threat of going through a number of freeze/thaw cycles. Make sure the bushes remain moist, but not too wet, throughout the winter months. Take the containers back out when it's safe to do so in spring.

Harvesting

Blueberries are ready for harvesting when they turn, not surprisingly, blue. Test one, and if it is sweet and tastes the way you expect, they are ready for harvest.

Tips

Gardeners are discovering that woody ornamentals and fruit-bearing shrubs can grow quite successfully in containers. Depending on where you are in Canada, you may have to go to some effort to overwinter the blueberry bushes so they survive and continue to thrive year after year, but having fresh blueberries at your fingertips is worth it.

Recommended

V. angustifolium var. *laevifolium* (low-bush blueberry, wild blueberry) is a low, bushy, spreading shrub with small, glossy, green leaves that turn red in fall. It grows 10–60 cm tall and spreads 30–60 cm. Clusters of small, bell-shaped, white or pink flowers are produced in spring, followed by small, round fruit that ripens to dark blue in midsummer. (Zones 2–8)

V. corymbosum (highbush blueberry) is a bushy, upright, arching shrub with green leaves that turn red or yellow in fall. It grows 90 cm–1.5 m tall with an equal spread. Clusters of white or pink flowers at the ends of the branches in spring are followed by berries that ripen to bright blue in summer. Several cultivars are available, including **'Bluecrop,'** with tart, light blue berries; **'Blueray,'** with large, dark blue berries; and **'Chippewa,'** with sweet, light blue berries. (Zones 3–8)

Problems and Pests

Rare problems with caterpillars, rust, scale, powdery mildew and root rot can occur.

A handy way to preserve blueberries is to spread them on a cookie sheet and put them in the freezer. Once they are frozen, they can be transferred into an air-tight bag and put back in the freezer. The berries will be frozen individually, rather than in a solid block, making it easy to measure out just what you need for a single recipe or serving.

Strawberries

Fragaria

Many strawberry plants, with their pretty little white flowers, spread vigorously by runners when grown in the ground. Long shoots spread out from the parent plant, and small baby plants grow at the tips. In containers the plants can't spread as far, but the runners continue to grow and produce an abundance of berries.

Starting

Some selections can be started indoors about 12 weeks before you plan to plant them outside. Other selections are only available as crowns or plants. Plant them outdoors, either directly into the ground or into containers, around the last frost date. They tolerate light frosts.

Growing

Strawberries grow well in **full sun** or **light shade.** The potting mix or soil should be **fertile, neutral to alkaline, moist** and **well drained**. They tolerate acidic soil but won't produce as much fruit.

Harvesting

Pick strawberries as soon as they are ripe. Some types produce a single large crop of fruit in early summer, and others produce a smaller crop throughout most or all of summer.

Tips

Strawberries make interesting, tasty and quick-growing groundcovers in raised beds. They do well in any type of container, including window boxes and hanging baskets. The selections that don't produce runners are also good for edging beds.

Recommended

F. chiloensis (Chilean strawberry), *F. vesca* (wild strawberry, alpine strawberry) and *F. virginiana* (Virginia strawberry) have been crossed to form many hybrids. Similar in appearance, they generally form a low clump of three-part leaves and may or may not produce

runners. Flowers in spring are followed by early to midsummer fruit. Some plants produce a second crop in fall, and others bear fruit all summer. The fruit of wild or alpine strawberries is smaller than the fruit of the other two species. Popular cultivars include mid-season producers **'Cabot'** and **'Kent'** and ever-bearing producers **'Sweetheart,' 'Temptation'** and **'Tristar.'** (Zones 3–8)

Problems and Pests

The fruit is susceptible to fungal diseases, so mulch to protect it. Some leaf spot, spider mite and wilt problems can occur.

The name strawberry has uncertain origin, perhaps originally being "strayberry" or "strewberry."

Basil

Ocimum

Of any herb, basil is probably the one that can be grown by every level of green thumb. There is an amazing array of selections to choose from in the basil family, and new introductions come out almost annually. The fragrant leaves of fresh basil add a delicious flavour to a wide variety of savory and sweet dishes, and it's no surprise that basil is one of the mainstays of cooking today.

Starting

Start seeds indoors about four weeks before the last frost date. Keep the potting mix moist, and the seeds should germinate within a week. Plant the seedlings out in spring after any risk of frost has passed. The other option is to start with young plants purchased from your local garden centre.

Growing

Basil grows best in **full sun** in a warm, sheltered location. The potting mix or soil should be **fertile, moist** and **well drained**. Pinch tips regularly to encourage bushy growth. Remove all flower spikes and fertilize with an organic fertilizer such as compost tea. You'll soon see fresh growth emerge.

If you choose to take your basil indoors to use throughout the colder months, place it in a location with as much natural light as possible, or under an artificial growing light. Make sure to pinch the newest growth back often to promote a stalky, bushy plant.

Harvesting

To use fresh basil in the kitchen, pinch out the newest tips throughout the growing season. As fall approaches, closely watch the weather forecasts; before the first fall frost, cut the leafy stalks at soil level, bring them indoors and hang them to dry. Store dried basil in airtight containers.

There is the possibility that mould could set in if the leaves take too long to dry. As an alternative to drying basil for storage, the leaves can be chopped finely and mixed with a little water, then frozen into ice cubes.

Tips

Although basil will grow best in a warm spot outdoors in the garden, it can be grown successfully in a pot by a bright window indoors to provide you with fresh leaves all year.

Recommended

O. basilicum is an annual that produces aromatic, lush green, sometimes purple-flushed foliage in a bushy form, 30–60 cm tall and 30–45 cm wide. Purple- or pink-tinged flowers are produced in spikes above the foliage. Although there are many species, hybrids and cultivars to choose from, the tender leaves of any type are easily damaged by both frost and lengthy periods of intense, direct sun. The following is only a small sample of what is available. **'Ararat'** bears purple-marked foliage with a strong hint of anise flavour. **'Cinnamon'** has purple-stained stems and distinctly veined foliage with a clean, spicy aroma with a hint of cinnamon. **'Compatto'** is a compact form of **'Genovese,'** and both are very flavourful standard large-leaf selections. **Var. minimum** (bush basil, Greek basil) is a dwarf selection with tiny, pungent leaves and white flowers. **'Spicy Globe'** is a uniform bush basil with larger leaves.

Problems and Pests

Basil is prone to spider mites, aphids, leafhoppers, Japanese beetles, root-knot nematodes and root rot.

Not all basil selections are suitable for cooking, as they may be too strong or bitter, overwhelming a dish rather than complementing it.

Basil is a good companion plant for tomatoes—both like warm, moist growing conditions, and when you pick tomatoes for a salad you'll also remember to include a few sprigs of basil.

Coriander and Cilantro

Coriandrum

Coriander is a multi-purpose herb. The leaves and seeds have distinct flavours and culinary uses. The leaves, called cilantro, are used in salads, salsas and soups. The seeds, called coriander, are used in pies, chutneys and marmalades. The seeds have also been used in breads and cakes, not only for their flavour but also because of the digestive action the seeds have on breaking down carbohydrates.

Starting

Cilantro can be started from seed or purchased as a seedling. It does not like to be transplanted, however, so try to minimize the number of times it will have to be moved. The seed should be sown thinly and covered with a very thin layer of soil.

Growing

Coriander prefers **full sun** but tolerates partial shade. The soil should be **fertile, light** and **well drained**. This plant dislikes humid conditions and does best during a dry summer.

If you're growing it primarily for cilantro, prevent the plant from flowering to produce the best leaf development. Dead-head regularly unless you plan on using the flowers. If you're growing the plants strictly for the coriander seeds, leave the flowers intact and try not to remove too much of the foliage, as the plant will need as much energy as possible to get to the seed stage.

The delicate, cloud-like clusters of flowers attract pollinating insects such as butterflies and bees as well as predatory insects that will help keep pest insects at a minimum in your garden.

Harvesting

Harvest the leaves throughout the growing season because they are most flavourful when used fresh. Choose the lower or older leaves for the strongest flavour. They can be frozen in ice-cube trays for use year round.

The stems can be eaten when young and tender. They should be stored stem down in water and covered with plastic until just before serving. The flowers are also flavourful, reminiscent of the leaves but sweeter. Pick the flowers as they open.

The seeds should be collected as soon as they ripen. A sure sign that they are ripe is when they turn brown and harden late in the season. Spread the seeds out to dry and then store them in an airtight container.

Both coriander and cilantro use dates back to Biblical times. Today they're commonly used in a variety of ethnic cuisines, including Mexican, Mediterranean, Cajun and Asian.

Tips

Coriander has pungent leaves and is best planted where people will not have to brush past it. It is, however, a delight to behold when in flower. Add a plant or two here and there throughout your garden, both for the visual appeal and to attract beneficial insects.

Recommended

C. sativum grows up to 60 cm tall and spreads 30–45 cm. It forms a clump of lacy basal foliage above which large, loose clusters of tiny, white flowers are produced. The seeds ripen in late summer and fall. **'Cilantro'** produces very flavourful foliage. **'Morocco'** is a fine selection for seed production.

Problems and Pests

Aphids and leafhoppers can pose a problem for cilantro plants, as can bacterial leaf spot and root-knot nematodes.

Chewing coriander seed is great for freshening your breath.

Parsley
Petroselinum

Although usually used as a garnish, parsley is rich in vitamins and minerals and is reputed to freshen the breath after garlic- or onion-rich foods are eaten. Parsley is one of the main components of the traditional *bouquet garni*, French for garnished bouquet, along with rosemary, thyme, bay leaves and peppercorns. This indispensable herb is easy to grow, harvest and use in everyday meals. Parsley is also a helpful companion to other plants in the garden, including roses and tomatoes, and when in flower, it attracts pollinating insects.

Starting

Parsley can be sown directly in the garden once the last frost date has passed or four to six weeks early indoors. If you start seeds early, use peat pots so the plants can be potted or planted out without disrupting their roots.

Parsley can be a little challenging to start from seed because it requires high temperatures for germination. The germination period can take weeks, and without consistent heat and moisture, most of the seed will not germinate successfully. Young plants are always available for transplanting and are often the best way to get started.

Growing

Parsley grows well in **full sun** or **partial shade**. The soil should be of **average to rich fertility, humus rich, moist** and **well drained**.

Parsley leaves can be fried and sprinkled over fish dishes for a little extra flavour and crunch.

Harvesting

Parsley can be cut and used fresh throughout the growing season. It is the most flavourful when used fresh. It can also be dried. It maintains its green colour even after drying and will keep for months. For freezing, chop fresh leaves finely, mix with a little water and freeze in ice-cube trays for later use.

Tips

Keep containers of parsley close to the house for easy picking, and bring them indoors to a sunny window to grow year-round. Use deep pots to allow this herb to develop a long, efficient taproot system.

Recommended

P. crispum (curly parsley) forms a clump of bright green, divided leaves. This plant is biennial, but it is usually grown as an annual. **'Champion Moss Curled'** has finely cut, curled leaves. **'Crispum'** is a strongly flavoured, crinkly leaved selection. **'Dark'** has very dark green leaves. **'Paramount'** bears tightly curled, dark green leaves. **Var. *tuberosum*** (Hamburg parsley) produces enlarged, edible roots. ***P. crispum neapolitanum*** (Italian parsley, French parsley) produces flat leaves with a stronger flavour.

Problems and Pests

Parsley is resistant to pests and diseases.

Parsley leaves make a tasty and nutritious addition to salads. Tear freshly picked leaves and sprinkle them over or mix them into your mixed greens.

Begonia

Begonia

With their beautiful flowers, compact habit and decorative foliage, there is sure to be a begonia to fulfill your shade-gardening needs.

Starting

Tuberous begonias can be purchased in late winter or early spring for planting. They can be started indoors until it's safe to take them outdoors. Tubers started in February should begin to bloom in June, and those started in March or early April should bloom sometime in July.

Start, or sprout, the tubers in a seed tray or box of damp potting mix in February or March. Space them roughly 5 cm apart and bury them deep enough that the top side is just slightly covered,

enough to remain moist. The top side can be identified by its concave appearance, while the bottom of the tuber sticks out a bit. The ideal temperature to start tuberous begonias is 18° C, but they can tolerate higher temperatures under grow lights.

Once the tubers have sprouted and small leaves are showing, gently remove the tubers from the potting mix and transplant them into larger pots, or if it is warm enough outside, plant them where they will remain for the rest of the growing season. Keep the sprouted tubers moist but not too wet, as they are prone to rot.

Tuberous begonias can also be planted as started plants purchased from the garden centre. They're abundantly available and will begin blooming earlier in the season than if you start them from scratch indoors.

Fibrous begonias (wax begonias) are best purchased as starter plants from the garden centre, as are the majority of begonia species and cultivars. Buying them already started allows you to get a jump on the season.

Growing

Light shade or partial shade is best, though some wax begonias tolerate full sun if the soil is kept moist. The potting mix or soil should be **neutral to acidic,**

fertile, rich in organic matter and **well drained**. Allow the soil to dry out slightly between waterings, particularly for tuberous begonias. Begonias love warm weather, so don't plant them out before the soil warms in spring; in cold soil, they may become stunted and fail to thrive.

Tips

All begonias are useful for shaded garden spaces. The trailing, tuberous varieties can be used in hanging baskets, where the flowers can cascade over the edges. Wax begonias have a neat, rounded habit that makes them particularly attractive as edging plants in decorative pots. For a great houseplant over winter, pot either type before the first fall frost.

Recommended

B. semperflorens (wax begonia) has pink, white, red or bicoloured flowers and green, bronze, reddish or white-variegated foliage.

B. x *tuberhybrida* (tuberous begonia) is generally sold as a tuber and is popular for its many shades of red, pink, yellow, orange or white flowers.

Problems and Pests

Begonias are susceptible to rot, if kept too wet for long periods of time. The tuberous selections are prone to aphids, powdery mildew and slugs.

Because wax begonias are generally pest free and bloom all summer even without deadheading, they are ideal flowers for the lazy gardener.

Geranium

Pelargonium

Tough, predictable, sun-loving and drought-resistant, geraniums have earned their place as flowering favourites in the annual garden. If you are looking for something out of the ordinary, seek out the scented geraniums, with their fragrant and often decorative foliage.

Starting

Geraniums can be started either with cuttings from last year's plants, from seed or from starter plants purchased from the garden centre. Geraniums are slow from seed, so start them early: in mid to late January. The seeds may need to soak overnight before sowing to soften the outer seed coats.

Grow your seedlings in full sun or under grow lights for roughly 12 to 14 hours daily. Once the plants are roughly the height of your index finger, pinch out the newest growth to maintain dense, bushy growth. When it's safe to plant outdoors, transplant into the containers where they'll remain for the remainder of the season. Your plants will begin blooming about 12 to 16 weeks after sowing.

Growing

Geraniums prefer **full sun** but tolerate partial shade, though they may not bloom as profusely. The potting mix should be **well drained**. Fertilize with quarter-strength fertilizer every one or two weeks during the growing season. Deadhead to keep geraniums blooming and looking neat, and pinch them back occasionally to keep plants bushy.

Tips

Very popular, geraniums make useful additions to borders, beds, planters, hanging baskets and window boxes. Although they are treated as annuals, they are actually perennials and can be kept indoors over winter in a bright room. In late winter, take cuttings from these indoor plants to start new plants for the coming season.

Recommended

P. peltatum (ivy-leaved geranium) has thick, waxy leaves and a trailing habit. Many cultivars are available.

P. zonale (zonal geranium) is a bushy plant with red, pink, purple, orange or white flowers and, frequently, banded or multi-coloured foliage. Many cultivars are available.

P. **species** and **cultivars** (scented geraniums, scented pelargoniums) are a large group of geraniums that are grown for their fragrant leaves. The scents are grouped into categories such as rose, mint, citrus, fruit, spice and pungent.

Problems and Pests

Geraniums are rarely affected by pests or diseases, but aphids can become a problem when populations are

excessively high. Rust can be common in certain parts of the country, but is easily remedied.

Ivy-leaved geranium is one of the most beautiful plants to include in a mixed hanging basket.

Petunia

Petunia

Planted alone, petunias' bushy growth will fill a container and spill over the edges with an abundance of colour. The rich shades of their flowers make them excellent companions for other flowering plants as well as for just about any other plant. Petunias are ideal for any container garden.

Starting

Petunias should be started indoors roughly 10 to 12 weeks before the last frost date. The seeds need light to germinate. Sprinkle seeds on moist seed mix and do not cover them with any soil. Place a clear plastic dome, or plastic wrap, over the seed tray to help maintain a moist environment for the seeds to germinate. Once the seeds have germinated, remove the covering and place the tray in a sunny location.

When the seedlings have a few sets of leaves, pinch out the tips to encourage

branching. The seedlings can be transplanted once they're a few inches tall, before the roots become too entangled to pull apart.

Growing

Petunias prefer **full sun**. The potting mix should be **moist** and **well drained**. Fertilize no more than monthly during the growing season with quarter-strength fertilizer. Pinch halfway back in mid-summer to keep plants bushy and to encourage new growth and flowers.

Tips

Use petunias in containers and hanging baskets. Any type of container will do, and petunias will thrive in just about any location as long as they have enough space, lots of sun and moist soil.

Recommended

P. x *hybrida* is a large group of popular, sun-loving annuals that fall into three categories. **Grandifloras** have the largest flowers in the widest range of colours, but they can be damaged by rain. **Millifloras** have the smallest flowers in the narrowest range of colours, but this type is the most prolific and least likely to be damaged by heavy rain. **Multifloras** bear intermediate-sized flowers that are only somewhat susceptible to rain damage.

Problems and Pests

Petunias are relatively free of pests and diseases. Aphids can become a problem, but usually only when populations are excessively high.

The rekindling of interest in petunias resulted largely from the development of many exciting new varieties. They are once again among the most popular and sought-after plants for the annual garden.

Black-Eyed Susan

Rudbeckia

Bright and cheerful, black-eyed Susan provides a summer-long display of colourful flowers.

Starting

Perennial *Rudbeckia* is one of the easiest plants to start from seed. If you are able to grow it in the ground, then seeding directly into the location where it will spend its life is best. However, if your black-eyed Susan will be grown in a container, it is probably best to begin with starter plants. This will ensure that you have flowers throughout most of the season, on a more robust, larger plant overall rather than waiting all season long for it to look like a worthy perennial.

Growing

Black-eyed Susan grows well in **full sun** or **partial shade**. The potting mix or soil should be **well drained**. Water regularly, though plants are fairly drought tolerant. Fertilize monthly with a half-strength fertilizer. Pinch plants in June to encourage shorter, bushier growth. Deadhead to keep the plants neat and to encourage more flower production.

Tips

Black-eyed Susan is a floriferous addition to mixed containers. It is good to use in themed containers such as wildflower or native containers, as it isn't unruly and won't become lank, floppy or messy, as some plants do if grown in containers. It's also great for borders and edging.

Recommended

R. hirta (gloriosa daisy) is a short-lived perennial that forms a bushy mound of bristly foliage and bears bright yellow,

As a cut flower, black-eyed Susan is long lasting in arrangements.

daisy-like flowers with brown centres from summer through to the first hard frost in fall. **'Becky'** is a dwarf cultivar that grows up to 30 cm tall and has large flowers in solid and multi-coloured shades of yellow, orange, red or brown. **'Cherokee Sunset'** was a 2002 All-America Selections winner. It bears semi-double and double flowers in all colours. **'Irish Eyes'** bears bright yellow flowers with green centres. This cultivar grows 60–75 cm tall and is best in larger containers where it will not look out of proportion. **Toto Series** is a group of bushy, dwarf cultivars that grow 30–40 cm tall and bear single flowers with central brown cones and golden orange, lemon yellow or rich mahogany petals. (Zones 2–8; often treated as an annual)

Problems and Pests

Black-eyed Susans are mostly unaffected by pests and diseases, except for bacterial leaf spot.

Coral Bells

Heuchera

From soft yellow-greens and oranges to midnight purples and silvery, dappled maroons, coral bells offer a great variety of foliage options for a perennial garden with partial shade.

Starting

Coral bells are difficult to sow as seed, but as starter plants, they're as easy as any other.

Growing

Coral bells grow best in **light shade** or **partial shade** and tolerate full sun, though some foliage colours may bleach out. Plants grow leggy in full shade. The potting mix or soil should be of **average to rich fertility, humus rich, neutral to alkaline, moist** and **well drained**. Good air circulation is essential. Deadhead to prolong blooming.

To overwinter coral bells, drop the moist potted plant into a large enough hole in the ground in fall, and mulch heavily with straw or bark mulch. Cut the foliage back to 2.5 cm above ground. Once the ground has thawed in spring, remove the pot and you're good to go.

Every three or four years, coral bells should be dug up and the oldest, woodiest roots and stems removed. Plants may be divided at this time, if desired, then replanted with the crown at or just above soil level.

Tips

Grown for their foliage more than their flowers, coral bells are useful individually or in groups in containers of any kind. Combine different foliage types for an interesting display.

Recommended

Coral bells are a mound-forming or spreading perennial that grows 30 cm–1.2 m tall and spreads 30–45 cm. There are many hybrids and cultivars available.

'**Caramel**' has apricot-coloured foliage and pink flowers. '**Chocolate Ruffles**' has ruffled, glossy, brown foliage with purple undersides that give the leaves a bronzed appearance. '**Coral Cloud**' forms a clump of glossy, crinkled leaves and bears pinkish red flowers. '**Firefly**' develops a clump of dark green leaves with attractive, fragrant, bright pinkish red flowers. '**Lime Rickey**' forms a low mass of chartreuse leaves. '**Marmalade**' has foliage that emerges red and matures to orange-yellow. '**Montrose Ruby**' has bronzy purple foliage with bright red undersides. '**Northern Fire**' has red flowers and leaves mottled with silver. '**Obsidian**' has lustrous, dark purple, nearly black, foliage. '**Pewter Veil**' has silvery purple leaves with dark grey veins. Its flowers are white flushed with pink. (Zones 3–8)

Problems and Pests

Coral bells are fairly resistant to most pests and diseases. Making sure they have good air circulation and good drainage are two of the best ways to keep your plants healthy.

Coral bells have a strange habit of pushing themselves up out of the soil because of their shallow root systems. If this happens, just tuck them back in.

Lavender

Lavandula

Lavender is considered the queen of herbs. With both aromatic and ornamental qualities, it makes a valuable addition to any sunny garden space.

Starting

Lavender isn't easy to grow from seed. Starter plants are much simpler and will provide you with flowers in the first year.

Growing

Lavender grows best in **full sun**. The soil or potting mix should be **average to fertile, alkaline** and very **well drained**. Once established, these plants are heat and drought tolerant.

Protect plants from winter cold and wind by locating them in a very sheltered spot or by burying the pot in the ground and mulching them in fall. Plants can be sheared in spring or after flowering.

Tips

Lavender is ideal for growing in containers of any kind. It can be planted individually, in groups of odd numbers or with other plants for contrast. Lavender is quite popular in herb pots, but when mixed with other complementary fragrant plants, your small urban space will become irresistible.

Recommended

L. angustifolia (English lavender) is a bushy, aromatic plant. It grows about 60 cm tall, with an equal spread. It bears spikes of light purple flowers from midsummer to fall. The many cultivars include plants with white or pink flowers, silvery grey to olive green foliage and dwarf or compact habits. (Zones 5–8)

L. x intermedia is a rounded shrub with aromatic, grey-green leaves and spikes of blue or purple flowers held on long stems. (Zones 5–8)

L. stoechas (French lavender) is a compact, bushy shrub with grey-green leaves and dark purple flower spikes. (Zone 8)

Problems and Pests

Lavender doesn't really suffer from pests or diseases. It can suffer from root rot, however, so make sure the potting mix or soil is very well drained and sandy.

Flowering Maple
Abutilon

Flowering maple is a vigorous shrub with beautiful flowers and decorative foliage, and it deserves a place in your urban garden.

Growing

Flowering maple grows well in **full sun** or **light shade**. The potting mix should be **moist** and **well drained**. Fertilize every two weeks during the growing season with quarter- to half-strength fertilizer. Trim it back annually to keep the size manageable.

In zones 4 and colder, this tender plant will not survive winter outdoors and will need to be brought into a space that is sheltered from the extreme cold. The space for overwintering should ideally be cool enough for the plant to go into dormancy; however, flowering maple will do fine as a houseplant indoors.

Tips

Flowering maple makes a stunning specimen, but it is also a lovely companion plant. Plant mounding and trailing annuals around the base of flowering maple to create a pretty display.

Recommended

A. x hybridum (flowering maple) is a tender, bushy shrub that grows 1.2–1.5 m tall and spreads 60–90 cm. It bears downy, maple-like leaves on woody branches. The single flowers are pendulous and bell shaped. There are a number of varieties available in a variety of colours including peach, white, cream, yellow, orange, red or pink. There are also several selections with variegated foliage. Some of the variegated selections bear very few flowers. **'Kentish Belle'** bears vibrant orange flowers. **'Nabob'** has crimson red flowers.

Problems and Pests

Flowering maple may experience problems with spider mites, aphids, thrips and rot if kept too wet for long periods.

Hydrangea

Hydrangea

From rounded shrubs and small trees to climbing vines, hydrangeas offer a wealth of possibilities for use in containers.

Growing

Hydrangeas grow well in **full sun** or **partial shade**, and some species tolerate full shade. These plants perform best in cool, moist conditions, and some shade will reduce leaf and flower scorch in hotter gardens. The potting mix should be **humus rich, moist** and **well drained**. Fertilize monthly during the growing season with quarter- to half-strength fertilizer. Move containers to a sheltered location out of the wind and sun in winter.

Tips

Hydrangeas will brighten up any mixed container, with their large flower clusters. Shrubby forms can be grown alone or combined with other plants. Tree forms are small enough to grow in containers but large enough to offer a good vertical accent. Climbing hydrangea can be grown in a large container and used to create a beautiful display against a wall or even over the edge of a balcony.

Recommended

H. anomala subsp. *petiolaris* (climbing hydrangea) is an elegant climbing plant with dark green, glossy leaves. It bears clusters of lacy-looking flowers in mid-summer. (Zones 4–8)

H. arborescens 'Annabelle' (Annabelle hydrangea) is a rounded shrub that bears large clusters of white flowers, even in shady conditions. (Zones 3–8)

H. macrophylla (bigleaf hydrangea) is a rounded shrub that bears flowers in shades of pink, red, blue or purple from mid to late summer. Many cultivars are available. (Zones 5–8)

H. paniculata 'Grandiflora' (Peegee hydrangea) is a spreading to upright large shrub or small tree that bears white flowers from late summer to early fall. (Zones 4–8)

H. quercifolia (oakleaf hydrangea) is a mound-forming shrub with attractive, cinnamon brown, exfoliating bark. Its large leaves are lobed like an oak's and turn bronze to bright red in fall. It bears conical clusters of sterile as well as fertile flowers. (Zones 4–8)

Problems and Pests

Hydrangeas are not prone to any problems or pests.

Weigela

Weigela

Weigelas have been improved through breeding, and specimens with more compact forms, longer flowering periods and greater cold tolerance are now available.

Growing

Weigelas prefer **full sun** but tolerate partial shade. The potting mix should be **well drained**. Fertilize monthly with half-strength fertilizer during the growing season. Move containers to a sheltered location protected from temperature fluctuations in winter.

Tips

With their green, bronze or purple foliage and long flowering period, weigelas can be used as focal points in mixed containers. Combine a purple-leaved weigela with a silver-leaved, white-flowered, trailing plant such as snow-in-summer to soften the edges of the container and to create a lovely contrast.

Recommended

W. florida is a bushy, spreading shrub with arching branches that bears clusters of dark pink flowers. It grows 30 cm–1.8 m tall and spreads 30 cm–1.2 m. Many hybrids and cultivars are available. Some of the best selections include 'Carnival,' with red, white or pink, thick, azalea-like flowers; MIDNIGHT WINE, a low, mounding dwarf with dark burgundy foliage; 'Polka,' with bright pink flowers; 'Red Prince,' with dark red flowers; 'Rubidor,' with yellow foliage and red flowers; 'Variegata,' with yellow-green variegated foliage and pink flowers; and WINE AND ROSES, with dark burgundy foliage and rosy pink flowers. (Zones 3–8)

Problems and Pests

Weigela is not prone to any problems or pests.

Weigela will become too large for a container after three to five years and should be moved to the garden when it does.

Asparagus Fern
Asparagus

Asparagus fern is not actually a fern but a member of the lily family and is closely related to edible asparagus. This lush, green plant fills the gaps where other plants don't and is often used as a trailing plant as well.

Growing

Asparagus fern grows best in **partial shade** or **light shade**, with protection from the afternoon sun. Avoid deep shade and direct sunlight. The potting mix should be kept evenly **moist**, but allowed to dry out a little between waterings. Fertilize weekly with quarter- to half-strength fertilizer during the growing season. It must be overwintered indoors or thrown away at the end of the season.

Tips

Vigorous growth makes asparagus fern a good filler plant for mixed containers, while its unique appearance and habit add an interesting visual element to any combination.

Recommended

A. densiflorus is an arching, tender perennial with light green, feathery, leaf-like stems. Two cultivars are commonly available. '**Myersii**' (foxtail fern) produces dense, 30–45 cm long, foxtail-like stems. '**Sprengeri**' (emerald fern) has bright green, arching to drooping stems and a loose, open habit. It spreads 90 cm–1.5 m and is often grown where it will have room to hang.

Problems and Pests

Asparagus ferns are not prone to pests or diseases.

Asparagus fern is a popular and common houseplant. It should be kept in bright but indirect light.

Elephant Ears
Colocasia

Elephant ears is a striking plant, and a fine contender for large containers to showcase its large, stunning leaves. It is customarily planted on its own as a specimen but is equally as interesting when planted with companions, particularly flowering annuals or perennials.

Growing

Elephant ears grow well in **light shade** or **full shade**. The potting mix should be **humus rich, slightly acidic** and **moist to wet**. This plant does well in boggy settings. Fertilize every two weeks during the growing season with quarter-strength fertilizer. Move elephant ears indoors in winter, or store the tuberous roots in a cool, dry location until spring.

Tips

Planted alone in a moist container or combined with other moisture-lovers, this plant makes a striking addition to any container garden.

Recommended

C. ecsulenta is a tuberous, warm-climate plant that produces a clump of large, heart-shaped leaves. It grows 60 cm–1.2 m tall with an equal spread. Cultivars with red- or purple-veined to dark purple or bronze foliage are available. **'Black Magic'** has dark purple leaves. **'Fontanesii'** has green leaves with red to purple stems, veins and margins.

Problems and Pests

Spider mites can be a problem for elephant ears.

Elephant ears are often included in water gardens and can actually be grown in up to 20 cm of water. Try them in a large water barrel if you want something other than miniature water lilies.

Plectranthus

Plectranthus

These mound-forming plants, with their often-aromatic foliage, eventually develop a more trailing habit. They're available in a variety of different foliage colours and paterns and create a beautiful complement to other plants within the same setting.

Growing

Plectranthus grows best in **light shade** or **partial shade**. The potting mix should be **moist** and **well drained**. Fertilize every two weeks during the growing season with quarter- to half-strength fertilizer.

Tips

These trailing plants make fabulous fillers for hanging baskets and mixed containers.

Place them near a walkway or other area where people will be able to brush past the plants and smell the spicy-scented foliage.

Recommended

P. argentatus is an upright to spreading plant with silvery green, hairy stems and leaves. It bears clusters of small, bluish white flowers near the ends of stems, in summer.

P. forsteri is a mounding, then trailing, plant with light green, slightly hairy leaves and clusters of small, white or pale purple flowers in summer. 'Marginatus' has cream-edged leaves.

P. madagascariensis (mintleaf) is a creeping, spreading plant with fleshy leaves that smell of mint when crushed. 'Variegated Mintleaf' has cream and green variegated leaves.

Problems and Pests

Plectranthus is not prone to any pests or diseases.

The trailing stems root easily from cuttings; start some in late summer to grow indoors through winter.

Appendix: Companion Plants

The following plants, arranged in alphabetical order by common name, all provide certain benefits to other plants when growing in proximity to each other, and/or to the garden in general.

Alliums (*Allium* spp.): group includes onions, garlic, leeks, shallots, chives and others; repel and distract slugs, aphids, carrot flies and cabbage worms

Asters (*Aster* spp.): general insect repellents

Borage (*Borago officinalis*): deters tomato worms; companion to tomatoes, squash and strawberries, improving growth and flavour

Calendula (*Calendula officinalis*): repels and distracts nematodes, beet leaf hoppers and other pests

Caraway (*Carum carvi*): loosens soil where it grows; attracts parasitic wasps and parasitic bees

Carrot (*Daucus carota*): attracts assassin bugs, lacewings, parasitic wasps, yellow jackets and other predatory wasps

Chamomile (*Chamaemelum nobile*): encourages other plants such as herbs, including lavender and rosemary, to increase their essential oil content

Chrysanthemums (*Chrysanthemum* spp.): reduce the number of nematodes

Cilantro/Coriander (*Coriandrum sativum*): scent repels aphids, attracts tachinid flies

Dill (*Anethum graveolens*): attracts hoverflies, wasps, tomato horn worms, honeybees, ichneumonid wasps, aphids, spider mites, squash bugs and cabbage looper

Fennel (*Foeniculum vulgare*): attracts ladybugs, syrphid flies and tachinid flies; repels and distracts aphids

Flax (*Linum usitatissimum*): deters potato bugs; companion to carrots and potatoes, improving growth and flavour

Geraniums (*Pelargonium* spp.): can be attractive to caterpillars, luring them away from adjacent plants

Horseradish (*Armoracia rusticana*): planted at corners of potato patch, will discourage potato bugs

Hyssop (*Hyssopus officinalis*): attracts honeybees and butterflies; repels and distracts cabbage moth larvae and cabbage butterflies

Larkspur (*Consolida ajacis*): protects vines against vine beetles

Lavenders (*Lavandula* spp.): general insect repellents; attract pollinating insects; provide protection against borers and mosquitoes

Lavender cotton (*Santolina chamaecyparissus*): general insect repellent

Lovage (*Levisticum officinale*): attracts ichneumonid wasps and ground beetles

Marigolds (*Tagetes* spp.): discourage beetles, nematodes and other pests

Mints (*Mentha* spp.): improve the flavour and growth of cabbage and tomatoes; deter white cabbage moths

Nasturtium (*Tropaeolum majus*): attracts predatory insects; repels and distracts cabbage loopers, squash bugs, white flies and cucumber beetles

Oregano (*Origanum vulgare*): repels and distracts aphids

Parsley (*Petroselinum crispum*): scent deters carrot flies

Peppers, hot (*Capsicum* spp.): produce a chemical that prevents root rot

Petunia (*Petunia* x *hybrida*): deters and distracts leafhoppers, Japanese beetles, aphids and asparagus beetles

Rue (*Ruta graveolens*): deters beetles in roses and raspberries; do not plant near cabbages, basil or sage

Sage (*Salvia officinalis*): deters cabbage moths and carrot flies

Tansy (*Tanacetum vulgare*): companion to roses and raspberries; deters flying insects, Japanese beetles, striped cucumber beetles, ants and squash bugs

Tomato (*Solanum lycopersicum*): when planted near asparagus, deters asparagus beetles

White alyssum (*Lobularia maritime*): reseeds frequently; helps to break up the soil, adding to organic content

Yarrow (*Achillea millefolium*): attracts predatory wasps, ladybugs, hoverflies and damselbugs

COMPANION PLANT RELATIONSHIPS

Plant	Compatible Plants	Incompatible Plants
apricots	basil, tansy	
asparagus	basil, parsley, tomatoes	
beans	most herbs and vegetables	beets, cabbage, garlic, kohlrabi, onions
beets	broccoli, cabbage, chard, garlic, kohlrabi, onions	beans
broccoli	beans, beets, celery, chamomile, cucumbers, lettuce, mint, onions, oregano, potatoes, thyme, rosemary	
cabbage	Alliums, aromatic herbs, beets, celery, chamomile, chard, spinach, potatoes	beans, corn, dill, parsnips, strawberries, tomatoes
carrots	Alliums, bell peppers, grapes, lettuce, peas, sage, tomatoes	dill, parsnips
cauliflower	beans, celery	strawberries

celery	beans, broccoli, cabbage, cauliflower, leeks, nasturtiums, onions, spinach, tomatoes	parsnips
chard, Swiss	beets, cabbage, lavender, onions	
corn	beans, cucumbers, melons, peas, potatoes, squash, tomatoes	cabbage
cucumbers	beans, broccoli, corn, lettuce, peas, sunflowers, radishes	aromatic herbs, potatoes
eggplant	beans, potatoes, spinach	
garlic	beets, lettuce, chamomile, parsnips, peaches, strawberries, tomatoes	beans, peas
grapes	basil, beans, carrots, geraniums, hyssop, peas	
kohlrabi	beets, onions	beans, tomatoes
leeks	carrots, celery, onions	
lettuce	broccoli, carrots, cucumbers, garlic, onions, radishes, strawberries	
melons	corn, radishes	
onions	beets, bell peppers, broccoli, cabbage, carrots, celery, chamomile, chard, kohlrabi, leeks, lettuce, tomatoes, strawberries	beans, peas
parsley	asparagus, tomatoes	
parsnips	beans, bell peppers, garlic, peas, potatoes, radishes	cabbage, carrots, celery
peaches	garlic, tansy	
peas	most herbs and vegetables	garlic, onions, potatoes
peppers, bell	carrots, onions, parsnips, tomatoes	
potatoes	beans, broccoli, cabbage, corn, eggplant, horseradish, marigolds, parsnips	cucumbers, peas, squash, sunflowers, tomatoes, turnips
radishes	cucumbers, lettuce, melons, nasturtiums, parsnips, peas	hyssop
spinach	cabbage, celery, eggplant, strawberries	
squash	corn, nasturtiums	potatoes
strawberries	beans, borage, garlic, lettuce, onions, spinach	cabbage, cauliflower
tomatoes	asparagus, carrots, celery, chives, corn, marigolds, nasturtiums, onions, parsley	cabbage, cucumbers, fennel, kohlrabi, potatoes
turnips	peas	potatoes

About the Author

Laura Peters is a certified Master Gardener, garden writer and photographer with over 30 gardening books to her credit. She has worked in almost every aspect of the horticultural industry in a career that has spanned more than 25 years. She is passionate about, and practices, organic gardening at every given opportunity. She is also an advocate of food security and community gardening, particularly in an urban setting. She loves to share her knowledge with fellow gardeners and environmentalists alike. She lives in Edmonton with her two cats, Blackie and Luna, and gardens both on her condominium balcony and in her parents' gardens just to mix it up with a variety of settings. Laura is inspired by nature and hopes you will be inspired to grow more of your own food, regardless of space, financial, time or skill restraints, because anything is possible and the rewards are priceless.